T0128246

A CHILD,
A SERVANT,
A KING

Shirley Ann Baxter Winders

WestBow
PRESS®
A DIVISION OF THOMAS NELSON
& ZONDERVAN

Scriptures are taken from the King James Bible.

WestBow Press books may be ordered through booksellers or by contacting:

WestBow Press
A Division of Thomas Nelson & Zondervan
1663 Liberty Drive
Bloomington, IN 47403
www.westbowpress.com
1 (866) 928-1240

ISBN: 978-1-9736-3180-4 (sc)
ISBN: 978-1-9736-3181-1 (hc)
ISBN: 978-1-9736-3179-8 (e)

Library of Congress Control Number: 2018907400

Print information available on the last page.

WestBow Press rev. date: 06/29/2018

Dedication

I dedicate this book to

A MAN I KNOW

A man I know whose body is weathered
His face is kissed by the sun
There is kindness in his eyes
And love in his heart

His smile is of joy and peace
His words are often spoken in tenderness
With love and compassion
Encouragement and hope

His hands are rough and hard
The hands of an honest man
Yet so soft and caring
With a tender touching hand

His knees have given way
With the wear and tear of his work
They have been replaced more than once
To give him another change to stand

His legs are tired and weak
His feet are growing thin
The soles are sore and painful
In this race he is trying to win

I know a man who is
A friend of love beyond measure
A husband above reproach
A sole mate forever

Called "Dad" by his children
A father who gave all
Called "teacher" by some
Called "Coach" by his team
Called "Grandpa" by his grandchildren

As teacher he taught many
The true Word of God
An example to all
In this life as he lives

A counselor when needed
A mentor always
A trainer, a survivor
Many hats he wore, changing as needed

He is a son, a brother, a husband, a father, a grandfather
Blessed, Caring, Gentle, Honest, Honorable,
Kind, Merciful, Prayful, Reliable, Thankful

By Shirley Ann Baxter Winders 2015 to my husband.

My husband, Fred Winders, who has encouraged and supported me from the very beginning.

To my children, Aaron, Brian, and Alisa whom I love dearly and want to share my love of God and encourage them never to give up in serving God. I hope my life has reflected the love of Jesus and how to live a life serving Him.

To my grandchildren, Macala, Jared, Hayley, Riley and Bailey; you are more precious than you will ever know.

I pray as you read this book that the words will reflect to you the unconditional love of God and what He has sacrificed for us. That your lives will grow deeper in the love for God and His plan for you.

Jesus said...

> "Greater love hath no man than this that a man lay down his life for his friends."
>
> (John 15:13; King James Version)

FOREWORD

I'm so proud of this book. It's written in a way that is easy to understand. All the points Shirley makes are supported by scripture.

There are areas that we all thought tradition instead of what the scripture says.

The biggest point is that we were never really taught in depth about the feasts of the Lord's, some felt they were feast of the Jews and not reverent today. In Genesis God tells Moses that they are His feasts and to be remembered. Take time to study them and what they mean, as you read her book it will be a tool to encourage and enlighten you in your study of the Bible. Well done Shirley.

Your loving husband
Fred Winders, Jr

EXPLANATION

Reading was one of my passionate desires, I enjoyed non-fiction as well as fiction. I would travel and visit distance and exciting places while still remaining in my comfort zone of home as I read books on travel and adventure. My first full job was at the Monroe County Library as librarian assistance to Miss Henze on the bookmobile in 1961–1966. What a great opportunity that was during my young adulthood years, to acquaint myself with authors and books; I had all the reading material I could ever dream of at my hands.

I have taught Sunday School Classes, helped in youth groups, and in 1966 I married my husband, and together; we have continued to teach classes, and lead youth groups in Florida and Indiana during our early years of marriage.

I have always had the desire to write my own book, so some years back I decided to write a book and loving non-fiction I chose to write on the subject I loved and taught, my Lord and Saviour Jesus Christ. But what could I write that had not already been told concerning the life of Jesus? So many books about His life, His childhood, His teachings, His miracles, His purpose, His Love; I could go on and on, there is no limit of subjects on His life. I started the book then laid it aside thinking this has all been wrote in previous books by many authors, what impact will my book have?

A few years ago there was a new teacher that came into our lives where we attend church; he was very knowledgeable of the Jewish customs and he would explain what the scripture meant in the Jewish customs. I had been teaching and studying the Bible for years and thought I was fairly knowledgeable but that was not the case. I realized there was much more to learn and the deeper I studied the more exciting God's Word became to me.

After class with Roger I would go home and dig into the Word, studying again what Roger taught in class. I would research his teachings, I begin to study Jewish customs and the Jewish way of life. Things were changing in my mind, the Bible was not just another book with Old Testament for Israel and New Testament for the church; but was a complete plan of God's time table for man's redemptive plan. I realized I knew very little concerning God's plan and wondered how many others were just like me, not realizing their knowledge of the Bible was a mere drop in the bucket as to what God really had for them.

I want to write telling God's plan of redemption and the design of God's plan. From the very beginning of time God knew man would sin and He designed a plan to save mankind. Why did God create man in the first place? He did not need man, He was not lonely; He had the fellowship of the Son and Holy Spirit and the angels, what more could He need.

> God that made the world and all things therein, seeing that he is Lord of heaven and earth, dwelleth not in temples made with hands;
> Neither is worshipped with men's hands, as though he needed anything, seeing he giveth to all life, and breath, and all things;
>
> (Acts 17:24-25)

> The LORD hath appeared of old unto me, *saying*, Yea, I have loved thee with an everlasting love: therefore with lovingkindness have I drawn thee.
>
> (Jeremiah 31:3)

> For we are his workmanship, created in Christ Jesus unto good works, which God hath before ordained that we should walk in them.
>
> (Ephesians 2:10)

God did not make us to be pawns in His hands, but gave us freedom of choice to choose between good and evil, to serve Him or serve Satan. In this book I have tried to show the plan and how God has given it to us. The crimson stream of blood flows from Genesis through Revelation; from when Adam and Eve fell in the garden to the end time when God will redeem us for His own and we will ever be caught up to be with our Lord.

I hope the pages of this book will reveal to you the true unconditional love of God for mankind and encourage you to live for Him. We do have a choice who we serve in this world today.

SHIRLEY ANN BAXTER WINDERS

INTRODUCTION

I'm writing this book because as I look back at the many ways we celebrated various holidays, I am beginning to see a difference between God's holy days—the feast of the Lords, and our traditional holidays. God's way of celebrating and our way of celebrating. Why did God send His Son, why did Jesus have to die? The plan of God is revealed in the Word of God, the Bible.

The more I study God's Word and the deeper I research I wonder at some of the things I did when I was a young person. It was tradition, I did what people around me did and celebrated the way they celebrated. I believed the way the people did and today we continue our traditions as did our ancestors. The more I study God's Word I realize my ways of celebrating were not always pleasing to God. I'm drawn back to these verses when I hear people talking about traditions.

> Thus have ye made the commandment of God of none effect by your tradition.
> *Ye* hypocrites, well did Esaias prophesy of you, saying,
> This people draweth nigh unto me with their mouth, and honoureth me with *their* lips; but their heart is far from me.
> But in vain they do worship me, teaching for doctrines the commandments of men.
> (Matthew 15:6-9)

"Tradition is often the enemy of truth. In spite of clear and convincing Scriptural and historical evidence, we often find that tradition replaces real truth with half-truths, fanciful stories, and wishful thinking, passed down through the centuries, from one generation to the next. Unfortunately, once tradition has taken hold, it can be very difficult to dislodge."

> Joseph Lenard, *Mysteries of Jesus' Life Revealed.* Truthinscripture.net 01/21/2017.

During the Christmas season the <u>traditional</u> nativity scene is brought out of storage, baby Jesus with Mary and Joseph, surrounded by the shepherds, animals, and three wise men are placed for all to admire. Is this ready the way it was?

I have always displayed my manger scene believing Jesus was born in a stable with animals. Traditions of our fathers has always played a huge part in my life, which have been pasted down from generation to generation. Sometimes traditions are fanciful stories pasted down from our ancestors just as Joseph Lenard stated in his quote, they are not always truthful.

My hope is this book will help us realize the real truth and better understand God's Word. God gave His Word to the Jews to instruct them how to live and serve Him. Jesus died to save the world from sin, He was a sacrifice for the entire world, Jews and Gentiles; but as Gentiles, if we don't understand the Jewish customs and ways it is hard to fully understand the Bible.

I use a lot of scripture in my book, but I want to back up what I say with God's Word. I use the King James Version, as I believe it is the nearest to the original Greek and Hebrew transcript. All other versions can be helpful in understanding at times, but they are mere translations of men and some leave out some of the main verses God would have us know.

Don't just take my word for what I have wrote, check out the scripture, search deep and let the Holy Spirit be your guide as you read. I hope this book brings you better understanding of God's promises and maybe answer some questions you may have had before reading.

SELAH

CHAPTERS

Chapter 1

THE FORERUNNER

His name was divinely given, it was to be "John" (Luke 1:13), meaning "Jehovah is gracious" in Hebrew.

John was known as "the Baptist" which means "an immerse "or one who administers the rite of immersion" (see Matthew 3:1; 11:11).

Jesus himself gave testimony of John saying, "Among them that are born of women there has not arisen a greater than John the Baptist". It was John who was to prepare the way of our Lord. (Isaiah 40:3, Malachi 3:1).

This man was of the priestly lineage of Aaron and though he came from the priestly line; John was not associated with the priesthood in Jerusalem, but was the last of the Old Testament prophets. A man devoted to God living in solitude in the wilderness until the time for his ministry. John was not connected to any social, political or religious group in Jerusalem, but he was anointed by the Holy Spirit in his mother's womb to be a master spokesman for our Lord.

Under the Levitical priesthood, the office of priesthood was handed down from father to son. Zacharias was a priest; therefore his son would be in the line of the Levitical priesthood.

When Rome began to rule in Israel and before the time of Jesus birth, the priesthood had become corrupt; the Roman Empire had begun to appoint men they wanted to be in the priesthood, who were not Levites, in fact the priest would actually buy their priesthood.

In the time of Christ, the Sadducees comprised most of the priesthood and were known to be a wealthy class of people, they were the aristocrats and held the majority of the seventy-one seats in the Sanhedrin. The Sadducees were more concerned with the politics than religion. The Pharisees were more like the middle class business men and were more in contact with the common man. Pharisees accepted the written Word of God (the Old Testament) but gave equal authority to oral tradition.

The chief priests, Caiaphas and Annas, were Sadducees and were instrumental in having Jesus crucified (John 18:13). During the time of Jesus the priesthood had become corrupt with Roman appointees and men buying their priesthood.

THE VISITOR IN THE TEMPLE

There was in the days of Herod, the king of Judaea, a certain priest named Zacharias, of the course of Abia: and his *wife* was of the daughters of Aaron, and her name was Elisabeth

And they were both righteous before God, walking in all the commandments and ordinances of the Lord blameless.

And they had no child, because that Elisabeth was barren, and they both were *now* well stricken in years

(Luke 1:5-7)

Zacharias, an elderly priest of the course of Abia, the eighth course, was awaiting for the casting of the third lot which determined who would offer incense. This was the most honorable part of the service in the daily ministry. There are said to have been twenty thousand priests in Christ's time, so that no priest would ever offer incense more than once in his life time. The lot fell on Zacharias and for the first and only time of his life he would offer the incense on the golden altar within the Holy Place in the temple.

The Jews tell us, that there were three priests employed for the service of the incense.

- One who carried away the ashes left on the altar at the preceding service.
- One who brought a pan of burning coals from the altar of sacrifice, having placed it on the golden altar they then departed.
- One who went in with the incense, sprinkled it on the burning coals and while the smoke ascended, made intercession for the people. This was the part that fell to Zacharias, and the most honorable part in the whole service.

I've often wondered about the <u>silence</u> in heaven mentioned in the book of Revelation. God specifically told Moses to pattern the tabernacle after the one in heaven. Would not the <u>services</u> conducted in the tabernacle also be patterned after the heavenly temple? Revelation 8:1-4 describes the exact same scene in the heavenly sanctuary.

> And when he had opened the seventh seal, there was <u>silence in heaven</u> about the space of half an hour.
>
> And I saw the seven angels which stood before God; and to them were given seven trumpets.
>
> And another angel came and stood at the altar, having a golden censer; and there was given unto him much incense, that he should offer *it* with the prayers of all saints upon the golden altar which was before the throne.
>
> And the smoke of the incense, *which came* with the prayers of the saints, ascended up before God out of the angel's hand.
>
> (Revelation 8:1-4)

OFFERING THE INCENSE

"The incensing priest and his assistance now approached first the altar of burnt-offering. One filled with incense a golden censer held in a silver vessel, while another placed in a golden bowl burning coals from the altar. As they passed from the court into the Holy Place, they struck a large instrument (called the 'Magrephah'), at sound of which the priests hastened from all parts to worship, and the Levites to occupy their places in the service of song; while the chief of the 'stationary men' ranged at the Gate of Nicanor such of the people as were to be purified that day. Slowly the incensing priest and his assistants ascended the steps to the Holy Place, preceded by the two priests who had formerly dressed the altar and the candlestick, and who now removed the vessels they had left behind, and, worshipping, withdrew. Next, one of the assistants reverently spread the coals on the golden altar; the other arranged the incense; and then the chief officiating priest was left alone within the Holy Place, to await the signal of the president before burning the incense. It was probably while thus expectant that the angel Gabriel appeared to Zacharias. As the president gave the word of command, which marked that 'the time of incense had come,' 'the whole multitude of the people without' withdrew from the inner court, and fell down before the Lord, spreading their hands in silent prayer."

Edersheim, Alfred. *The Temple: Its Ministry and Services as they were at the Time of Jesus Christ.* (Peabody, MA: Hendrickson Publishers, 1994)

When the offering of incense was made, everyone was quiet and spent time in prayer. In the story of Zacharias, "the whole multitude of the people were praying without the temple at the time of incense" (Luke 1:10). All was quiet while God received the prayers of the saints. The time required for the offering of incense was about half an hour. This explains the silence in heaven mentioned in (Revelation 8:1).

It was there in the Holy Place where the angel, Gabriel, appeared standing on the right side of the altar of incense; he spoke to Zacharias the message that Elisabeth would bare a son and they were to call him John. Zacharias doubted the angel and ask for a sign, the sign itself became a punishment for his unbelief, and when Zacharias came out of the temple he could not speak to the people. As soon as his course of service was over he returned to his own home (Luke 1:18:23).

MARY AND ELISABETH

Zacharias returned to his home in the hills of Judaea to his wife, Elisabeth, who was also the daughter of a priest. To be a priest was a great honor but to be married to the daughter of a priest was considered a double honor. Elisabeth conceived and hid herself five months; the Scripture does not tell us why Elisabeth hid herself. She may have decided to keep her pregnancy a secret until such a time that it was obvious she was with child and thus dispel any doubts. Perhaps since she had been looked upon for so many years with disgrace because of her barren condition; determined that no one should see her until they could look on her with favor, and see how the she had the fullest proof of God's blessing. Her reproach of being barren was taken from her and God was blessing them with a son in their old age.

> And thou shalt have joy and gladness; and many shall rejoice at his birth.
> For he shall be great in the sight of the Lord, and shall drink neither wine nor strong drink; and he shall be filled with the Holy Ghost, even from his mother's womb.
> And many of the children of Israel shall he turn to the Lord their God.
>
> (Luke 1:14-16)

To take the Nazarite vow meant a person did not drink alcoholic beverages and did not shave or cut their hair (Num. 6:1-5). This implies that John was dedicated to God throughout his life, even starting in his mother's womb.

Elisabeth believed God would perform a miracle and give to her and Zacharias a son whom they would name John, just as He promised by the angel Gabriel. Now when Elisabeth was pregnant with John, Gabriel made another visit to a young girl named Mary who was highly favored by God. Gabriel said to Mary:

> And the angel came in unto her, and said, Hail, *thou that art* highly favoured, the Lord *is* with thee: blessed *art* thou among women.

And when she saw *him*, she was troubled at his saying, and cast in her mind what manner of salutation this should be.

And the angel said unto her, Fear not, Mary: for thou hast found favour with God.

And, behold, thou shalt conceive in thy womb, and bring forth a son, and shalt call his name JESUS.

He shall be great, and shall be called the Son of the Highest: and the Lord God shall give unto him the throne of his father David:

And he shall reign over the house of Jacob for ever; and of his kingdom there shall be no end. Then said Mary unto the angel, How shall this be, seeing I know not a man?

And the angel answered and said unto her, The Holy Ghost shall come upon thee, and the power of the Highest shall overshadow thee: therefore also that holy thing which shall be born of thee shall be called the Son of God.

And, behold, thy cousin Elisabeth, she hath also conceived a son in her old age: and this is the sixth month with her, who was called barren.

For with God nothing shall be impossible.

And Mary said, Behold the handmaid of the Lord; be it unto me according to thy word. And the angel departed from her.

(Luke 1:28-38)

Mary arose and went with <u>haste</u> to the hill country of Judea to the home of Zacharias and Elisabeth; she <u>greeted</u> Elisabeth and stayed there three months. The Greek uses the noun *spoude*, which can mean "haste, speed," but also can carry the idea of "eagerness, diligence, enthusiasm, zeal.

The Greek word is *aspazomai*, for "greet." For the Jews greeting is an important ceremony; Jesus instructs his disciples to offer a greeting of "Peace to you," as they entered into homes. This word of peace, when received, functioned like a powerful blessing upon the home.

Why did Mary go to Elisabeth, She no doubt was excited, and eager to talk with Elisabeth about what both were experiencing at this time in their lives.

While we don't know the greeting Mary said to Elisabeth, it had an effect so powerful that Elisabeth was filled with the Holy Spirit, and began to speak out prophetically. "When Elisabeth heard Mary's greeting, the baby leaped in her womb, and Elisabeth was filled with the Holy Spirit." John the Baptist, in Elisabeth's womb responded to the presence of the Messiah inside of Mary.

> And it came to pass, that, when Elisabeth heard the salutation of Mary, the babe leaped in her womb; and Elisabeth was filled with the Holy Ghost:
>
> And she spake out with a loud voice, and said, Blessed *art* thou among women, and blessed is the fruit of thy womb.
>
> And whence *is* this to me, that the mother of my Lord should come to me?
>
> For, lo, as soon as the voice of thy salutation sounded in mine ears, the babe leaped in my womb for joy.
>
> And blessed is she that believed: for there shall be a performance of those things which were told her from the Lord.
>
> (Luke 1:41-45)

Mary and Elisabeth no doubt told each other of the angel's visits and the message the angel gave to them concerning the birth of their child. These two women were chosen by God, one past child bearing age; the other a young virgin, at the prime of child bearing age, probably in her teens and had never known a man. Both pregnant by a miracle of God and the Holy Spirit. Interestingly enough they are relatives whom God chose to be human instruments for the birth of two very unusual men, whose lives would turn the world upside down.

> And Mary abode with her about three months, and returned to her own house.
>
> (Luke 1:56)

Mary had beyond a doubt been an encouragement to Elisabeth and Zechariah as they were to her; I think God had planned the visit for Mary's benefit. Upon returning home, Mary would be subject to slander, here she was safe.

Once home, Mary would have to stand on her own spiritual feet, lonely, misunderstood, and rejected. Here she was loved, understood, and accepted.

Elisabeth gave birth to John and they named him as the angel had instructed Zacharias while talking to him in the temple. John's childhood is silent nothing is recorded in the scriptures of his early life. The Scriptures are silent as to the deaths of John's parents — nevertheless Jewish legend has it that Zacharias was slain by Herod the Great, for refusing to tell him where Elisabeth had fled to with her babe into the wilderness area of Judea, when he was trying to kill all the babies around Bethlehem. If the legend is true, we do not know, I don't find anything in the Bible that confirms the legend. Luke does say of John: "And the child grew, and waxed strong in spirit, and was in the deserts till the day of his showing unto Israel" (Luke 1:80). This desert area stretches from Jerusalem and Bethlehem eastward some 20 miles down to the Jordan River and the Dead Sea; it is a barren region of rugged hills and valleys.

MINISTRY OF JOHN THE BAPTIST

There was no further mention of John until the day he starts his ministry in the wilderness. John was thirty years old when he began his ministry; the age God required the Levites to be for service in the Temple.

> From thirty years old and upward even until fifty years old, all that enter into the host, to do the work in the tabernacle of the congregation.
>
> (Numbers 4:3)

Now Zacharias, the father of John was a priest in the Levitical priesthood, which was handed down from father to son

Why was John not serving in the temple at Jerusalem, why was he not a priest following in his father's footsteps? John was a special man with a specific purpose fulfilling God's call on his life; for now John was following the calling of God on his life. Remember the priesthood had become corrupt during the period when Israel was controlled by the Romans, God had other plans for John.

The voice of him that crieth in the wilderness, Prepare ye the way of the LORD, make straight in the desert a highway for our God.

(Isaiah 40:3)

As it is written in the prophets, Behold, I send my messenger before thy face, which shall prepare thy way before thee.

The voice of one crying in the wilderness, Prepare ye the way of the Lord, make his paths straight.

(Mark 1:2-3)

Now in the fifteenth year of the reign of Tiberius Caesar, Pontius Pilate being governor of Judaea, and Herod being tetrarch of Galilee, and his brother Philip tetrarch of Ituraea and of the region of Trachonitis, and Lysanias the tetrarch of Abilene,

Annas and Caiaphas being the high priests, the word of God came unto John the son of Zacharias in the wilderness.

And he came into all the country about Jordan, preaching the baptism of repentance for the remission of sins;

As it is written in the book of the words of Esaias the prophet, saying, The voice of one crying in the wilderness, Prepare ye the way of the Lord, make his paths straight.

Every valley shall be filled, and every mountain and hill shall be brought low; and the crooked shall be made straight, and the rough ways *shall be* made smooth;

(Luke 3:1-5)

When we count fifteen years after the start of Tiberius Caesar's reign, *(AD 14 to AD 37)* we arrive at AD 29 maybe as late as AD 30. When John the Baptist appears on the pages of scripture he is preaching the "kingdom of heaven" is at hand. John was preparing the people for the coming of the Messiah. He was God's man at God's *appointed time* to prepare the way for the coming king. Ancient history tells us that when a king, governor, or someone of importance came to visit, road crews were sent out to prepare the roads for their coming.

The roads were literally straightened, potholes were filled, rocks and debris were removed, and the roads were smoothed to create a smooth entry for the king. John was calling people to straighten their spiritual lives, to repent and stop sinning, change their hearts and lives. He fulfilled the prophecy of the voice crying in the wilderness spoken of in Isaiah 40:3-4

THE PROMISE

O Thou Bethlehem, City of David and birth place of our Saviour.

> And I will put enmity between thee and the woman, and between thy seed and her seed; it shall bruise thy head, and thou shalt bruise his heel.
>
> (Genesis 3:15)

In conception the seed comes from the male, however God's Word clearly states "Her seed", the woman's seed. Eve was deceived by the serpent and she ate of the forbidden fruit, Adam was not deceived but willingly ate of the fruit that Eve gave him and he knew he disobeyed God. He had a choice between obeying God and losing his partner or disobeying and remaining with the woman. It speaks of her seed (the seed of a woman) not his or theirs but the woman's seed. Deliverance would come from a woman without the aid of a man. All through the Bible we have scripture and signs that point to the birth of one who is to be our deliverer. He must be holy, His blood must be pure, without sin. We know all children (includes ALL descendants, you and me) of Adam and Eve are sinners because of Adam's fall, our blood is tainted with sin.

> For Adam was first formed, then Eve.
> And Adam was not deceived, but the woman being deceived was in the transgression.
>
> (1 Timothy 2:13-14)

God is omniscient and He knows the future. So He definitely knew that Adam and Eve would sin. But He created them anyway and gave them a free will with which they choose to sin.

O LORD, thou hast searched *me*, and known me.

Thou knowest my downsitting and mine uprising, thou understandest my thought afar off.

Thou compassest my path and my lying down, and art acquainted *with* all my ways.

For *there is* not a word in my tongue, *but*, lo, O LORD, thou knowest it altogether.

Thou hast beset me behind and before, and laid thine hand upon me.

Such knowledge is too wonderful for me; it is high, I cannot *attain* unto it.

(Psalm 139:1-6)

Declaring the end from the beginning, and from ancient times *the things* that are not *yet* done, saying, My counsel shall stand, and I will do all my pleasure:

(Isaiah 46:10)

God spoke to the prophet Isaiah concerning this promise.

Therefore the Lord himself shall give you a sign; Behold, a virgin shall conceive, and bear a son, and shall call his name Immanuel.

(Isaiah 7:14)

Immanuel means "*God with us.*" This child would be born of a virgin (an unmarried women) the seed of a woman. He would be conceived by the Holy Spirit, not man, his blood would be pure and free from sin. The bloodline comes from the father, so Joseph could not be Jesus father, Jesus had to have pure blood, that's why He was conceived by the Holy Spirit and not man. The Jewish people called this promised Saviour "*the Messiah.*" In Greek He is called "*the Christ.*"

For unto us a child is born, unto us a son is given: and the government shall be upon his shoulder: and his name shall be called Wonderful, Counsellor, The mighty God, The everlasting Father, and The Prince of Peace.

(Isaiah 9:6)

And thou, O tower of the flock, the strong hold of the daughter of Zion, unto thee shall it come, even the first dominion; the kingdom shall come to the daughter of Jerusalem.

(Micah 4:8)

OUR MESSIAH IS AN ETERNAL BEING

But thou, Bethlehem Ephratah, *though* thou be little among the thousands of Judah, *yet* out of thee shall he come forth unto me *that is* to be ruler in Israel; whose goings forth *have been* from of old, from everlasting.

(Micah 5:2)

"In the beginning was the Word, and the Word was with God, and the Word was God." …"And the Word was made flesh, and dwelled among us…"

(John 1:1, 14)

Now in the land of Israel there was a Jewish man by the name of Joseph, he was of the lineage of David as recorded in Matthew 1; a well-respected, honorable, and faithful man. Joseph was a skilled carpenter in Nazareth of Galilee and a man of faithful obedience to God whom God chose for a special purpose. He was pledged to be the husband of a young girl, whose name was Mary.

Mary was also a descendant of King David and her genealogy is found in Luke 3:23-38 (genealogy of Jesus). A young Jewish girl, preparing for marriage to Joseph; suddenly her life was about to change when God sent the angel, Gabriel to visit her. She was highly favored by God and would be the mother of God's only Son (the Messiah).

Chapter 2

THE BIRTH AND FULFILLMENT

Six months had passed since Zacharias was in the temple and the angel, Gabriel, appeared to him. Elisabeth was in her sixth month of pregnancy and God again sent the angel, Gabriel, to a young virgin in the city of Nazareth in Galilee.

Mary was espoused to a man named Joseph. The marriage covenant had been established and Mary was set apart exclusively to be his bride. *(Do you know the church is Jesus's Bride?)* Joseph had left to prepare a place for his bride to be, normally this would be about a year according to the Jewish weddings. During the period of separation the bride would gather her trousseau and prepare for married life. Mary was going about her daily duties of preparing for her life with Joseph, and Joseph, the bridegroom occupied himself with preparation of living accommodations for him and his bride. *(Jesus is preparing our place for His Bride as we prepare our lives for His services)*

At this point in their lives they were considered bound to each other same as in marriage, only a bill of divorcement could break their contract. During the time of agreement to marry and the actual marriage, they did not see each other as each one prepared for their wedding.

Puzzled at the appearance of the angel, Mary questioned, but she did not doubt as Zacharias had in his visit with Gabriel.

> Now the birth of Jesus Christ was on this wise: When as his mother Mary was espoused to Joseph, before they came together, she was found with child of the Holy Ghost.
>
> Then Joseph her husband, being a just *man*, and not willing to make her a publick example, was minded to put her away privily.
>
> But while he thought on these things, behold, the angel of the Lord appeared unto him in a dream, saying, Joseph, thou son of David, fear not to take unto thee Mary thy wife: for that which is conceived in her is of the Holy Ghost.
>
> And she shall bring forth a son, and thou shalt call his name JESUS: for he shall save his people from their sins.
>
> Now all this was done, that it might be fulfilled which was spoken of the Lord by the prophet, saying,
>
> Behold, a virgin shall be with child, and shall bring forth a son, and they shall call his name Emmanuel, which being interpreted is, God with us.
>
> Then Joseph being raised from sleep did as the angel of the Lord had bidden him, and took unto him his wife:
>
> And knew her not till she had brought forth her firstborn son: and he called his name JESUS.
>
> (Matthew 1:18-25)

Then said Mary unto the angel, How shall this be, seeing I know not a man?

And the angel answered and said unto her, The Holy Ghost shall come upon thee, and the power of the Highest shall overshadow thee: therefore also that holy thing which shall be born of thee shall be called the Son of God.

> And, behold, thy cousin Elisabeth, she hath also conceived a son in her old age: and this is the sixth month with her, who was called barren.
>
> For with God nothing shall be impossible.
>
> And Mary said, Behold the handmaid of the Lord; be it unto me according to thy word. And the angel departed from her.
>
> (Luke 1:34-38)

According to the writer of Luke, Mary was a cousin of Elisabeth, the wife of Zechariah the priest of the division of Abijah. Elisabeth was part of the lineage of Aaron and so of the tribe of Levi. Some of those who consider that the relationship with Elisabeth was on the maternal side, consider that Mary, like Joseph, to whom she was betrothed, was of the House of David and so of the Tribe of Judah, and that the genealogy of Jesus presented in Luke 3 from Nathan, third son of David and Bathsheba, is in fact the genealogy of Mary. The genealogy from Solomon given in Matthew 1 is that of Joseph. (Aaron's wife Elisheba was of the tribe of Judah, so all their descendants are from both Levi and Judah.)

THE TIME AND THE PLACE

> And it came to pass in those days, that there went out a decree from Caesar Augustus, that all the world ((*pasan tēn oikoumenēn means all the Roman Empire*) should be taxed. (*this was rather a census or enrollment being taken for taxing later*).
>
> (And this taxing was first made when Cyrenius was governor of Syria.)
>
> And all went to be taxed, every one into his own city.
>
> And Joseph also went up from Galilee, out of the city of Nazareth, into Judaea, unto the city of David, which is called Bethlehem; (because he was of the house and lineage of David:)
>
> To be taxed with Mary his espoused wife, being great with child.

> And so it was, that, while they were there, the days were accomplished that she should be delivered.
>
> And she brought forth her firstborn son, and wrapped him in swaddling clothes, and laid him in a manger; because there was no room for them in the inn.
>
> (Luke 2:1-7; my emphasis)

We know from history that an Empire-wide citizen registration took place for the award of the *Pater Patriae* upon Augustus in early 2 B.C.E., this was the census mentioned in Luke.

"The correct identity of Luke's registration has been a longstanding puzzle to historians. Recently Dr. Ernest Martin suggested that it was an oath of allegiance made on the occasion of Augustus' Silver Jubilee in 2 B.C. (see Chapter 5 of the second edition of his book). On February 5th of that year, Augustus was awarded the title "Pater Patriae," Father of the Country, in a year of celebrations, that commemorated the 750th anniversary of the legendary founding of Rome as well as Augustus' 25th year of rule."

ASKELM.com/star *"The Star of Bethlehem"*, chapter 12

If Luke's registration was Augustus' loyalty oath we can understand why both Joseph and Mary went specifically to Bethlehem. Joseph, being of the house and lineage of David, went to the city of David, which is Bethlehem, while everyone else went into his own city. As a descendent of David he was obliged to return to Bethlehem along with other claimants to the throne of Israel; under Jewish law the right to kingship could pass to Mary's descendants and so she also had to accompany her husband. This answers why Mary had to go to Bethlehem with Joseph.

Luke 2:6 makes it clear that Joseph and Mary were in Bethlehem for an unspecified number of days before Mary gave birth.

> And so it was, that, while they were there, the <u>days</u> were accomplished that she should be delivered.
>
> (Luke 2:6)

Bethlehem is located about five miles south of Jerusalem in the hills of Judea. Often called the City of David and also The House of Bread, this is where King David was born and where he cared for the family sheep in and around the hills of Bethlehem.

> And there were in the same country shepherds abiding in the field, keeping watch over their flock by night.
>
> And, lo, the angel of the Lord came upon them, and the glory of the Lord shone round about them: and they were sore afraid.
>
> And the angel said unto them, Fear not: for, behold, I bring you good tidings of great joy, which shall be to all people.
>
> For unto you is born this day in the city of David a Saviour, which is Christ the Lord.
>
> And this *shall be* a sign unto you; Ye shall find the babe wrapped in swaddling clothes, lying in a manger.
>
> (Luke 2:8-12)

THE TIME

The Bible gives us clues to the exact day of Jesus birth. The Gospel of Luke says John the Baptist was baptizing, John was born around the time of Passover, if not on Passover (Nisan, in the spring) and Jesus was born six months later. That places His birth in the month of Tishri in the early fall.

> Now in the fifteenth year of the reign of Tiberius Caesar, Pontius Pilate being governor of Judaea, and Herod being tetrarch of Galilee, and his brother Philip tetrarch of Ituraea and of the region of Trachonitis, and Lysanias the tetrarch of Abilene,
>
> Annas and Caiaphas being the high priests, the word of God came unto John the son of Zacharias in the wilderness.
>
> (Luke 3:1-2)

Now when all the people were baptized, it came to pass, that Jesus also being baptized, and praying, the heaven was opened,

And the Holy Ghost descended in a bodily shape like a dove upon him, and a voice came from heaven, which said, Thou art my beloved Son; in thee I am well pleased.

And Jesus himself began to be about thirty years of age, being (as was supposed) *the son* of Joseph, which was *the son* of Heli,

(Luke 3:21-23)

If Jesus was thirty years old near the commencement of the 15th year of Tiberius Caesar reign which was AD 27-28 this would place Christ's birth in 3 BC. Next look at Revelation 12:1- 5

And there appeared a great wonder in heaven; a woman clothed with the sun, and the moon under her feet, and upon her head a crown of twelve stars:

And she being with child cried, travailing in birth, and pained to be delivered.

And there appeared another wonder in heaven; and behold a great red dragon, having seven heads and ten horns, and seven crowns upon his heads.

And his tail drew the third part of the stars of heaven, and did cast them to the earth: and the dragon stood before the woman which was ready to be delivered, for to devour her child as soon as it was born.

And she brought forth a man child, who was to rule all nations with a rod of iron: and her child was caught up unto God, and *to* his throne.

(Revelation 12:1-5)

Some believe that Jesus was born during the Feast of Tabernacles because in John's Gospel he says *"tabernacled (Greek) among us"* (John 1:14). Tabernacles in the year 3 BC was from September 26 to October 3 BC. There is clear proof that Jesus' birth could not have been at any of the three holy days of Passover, Pentecost or Tabernacles. All Jewish men were required by biblical law to be in Jerusalem (Deuteronomy 16:6, 11, 16) during these feasts and Luke tells us that during the time of Jesus' nativity "everyone went into his own city" (Luke 2:3). Joseph and Mary were in Bethlehem when Jesus was born. The advancements in Astronomy and all biblical correlations has now made it possible to know the date of Jesus birth.

"Due to the work of Johannes Kepler (1571–1630), one of the great mathematical minds of human history, we can now find the Star today, with computer software that uses Kepler's equations NASA can now create sky maps of 1000's of year in the past.

Ernest L. Martin, a historian consulted NASA lunar-phase tables and found the image of the heavens described in Revelation 12:1-2. This sign occurred during a sixty minute period on September 11, 3 BC between sunset at 6:15 and 7:45."

ASKELM.com/star, *The Star of Bethlehem*", chapter 5

The Star of Bethlehem: The Star that Astonished the World, by Dr. Ernest L. Martin is a book well worth reading.

"On **September 11, 3 BC** the constellation Virgo (the virgin) appeared in Israel clothed with the sun and the moon at her feet from **6:18 pm to 7:39 pm.** This happened to occur at the beginning of the Feast of Trumpets; which is on the first day of the seventh month on the Jewish calendar."

ASKELM.com/star *The Star of Bethlehem*", chapter 5

September 11, 3 BC between 6:15pm-7:45pm, was the date of our Saviour's birth, on the Lord's feast day, Feast of Trumpets/Rosh Hashanah; according to the Revelation 12:1-5.

THE PLACE AND THE SHEPHERDS

Roman Emperor Constantine, built a Basilica over a cave in the 4th Century at the request of his mother, Helena. This is believed by many to be the birth place of Jesus. It was destroyed and the present basilica was built by Emperor Justinian in AD 530. This is a traditional believe, so what does the Bible say?

Clearly the Gospels of Matthew, Luke and John confirm Jesus was born in Bethlehem, but where in Bethlehem was Jesus born? The New Testament does not tell us the exact place nor does it record Jesus was born in a stable where donkeys and cows were kept. It just specifically says Jesus was laid in a manger in Bethlehem. "manger" refers to a trough where animals are fed. The Greek word which is translated in our Bibles is *Yatnh phat-ne (pronounced fat"-nay)*. The question is what kind of animals were fed and housed there. I believe the Old Testament reveals the birthplace of Jesus and history tells us what was housed there.

> And thou, O tower of the flock, the strong hold of the daughter of Zion, unto thee shall it come, even the first dominion; the kingdom shall come to the daughter of Jerusalem.
>
> (Micah 4:8)

In biblical times the city of Bethlehem was a greater area than it is today. The Tower of the Flock was in the city. Migdal Eder was known as the "Tower of the Flock" located just on the out skirts of Bethlehem today; was a watchtower where the birthing of the sacrificial lambs for the temple were born. The lambs were wrapped in swaddling clothes to protect them from harm after being born. These lambs had to be free from blemishes, because they were sacrificed for the sins of the people of Israel. You can read in the book of Leviticus chapter 1, God commands that the sacrifices had to be without blemishes.

The Life and Times of Jesus the Messiah by Alfred Edersheim has a lot of history and culture on the Jews and Israel. In this book the author talks about Migdal Eder and what took place there around Bethlehem.

> Edersheim, Alfred. "*The Life and Times of Jesus the Messiah*". Hendrickson Publishers, 1993.

Was it a coincidence that Jesus may have been born at Migdal Eder? Things don't just happen with God, He has a plan and He carries out His plan. He has appointments and He meets those appointments. Study the feasts of the Lord's, they are His appointments and Jesus has fulfilled the first four out of seven and He will fulfil the last three, more on these later.

Who were the shepherds that visited the babe in the manger? They were the priestly shepherds that cared for the flocks that were destined to be the temple sacrificial lambs. They were the shepherds from "Migdal Edar" at Bethlehem and they were specifically trained for this royal task of caring for these special flocks. They were not ordinary shepherds; these shepherds were under special Rabbinical care and trained to care for the lambs that were sacrificed in the temple.

The lower level of the tower of Migdal Eder was used as the birthing room for the sacrificial lambs. These priestly shepherds strictly maintained a ceremonially clean birthing place and when the lambs were born they were "wrapped in swaddling bands" to prevent them from harming themselves and placed in a hewn limestone rock known as "the manger". The original Greek text stated THE, but was translated in the King James Bible as A manger.

It was not just A manger but THE manger, and the shepherds would know THE manger was where the sacrificial lambs were birthed.

The term *definite article* refers to the word "the". In English we also have an *indefinite article*, "a" (or "an" before words beginning with vowels.)

In Greek there is no indefinite article. You will have to allow the context to tell you whether or not to supply an indefinite article in your English translation. But Greek does have a definite article.

According to the Thayer Greek Dictionary, this Greek word is defined as "the definite article" - **"the"** in its masculine, feminine or neuter gender, the demonstrative pronoun. The angels gave the shepherds two signs on where to find Jesus, these shepherds understand these signs.

I like this because…

- It places Jesus' birth in the location where the Passover lambs were born.
- It explains how the shepherds knew where to go to find the newborn babe and why "swaddling clothes" and "the manger" would be a significant sign.

- It explains why those shepherds were notified. Their calling was to certify the Passover lambs upon birth.

(Of all the mangers in Bethlehem what other manger would have swaddling clothes and what other manger would be called **THE** manger?) Tradition has us believe Joseph and Mary had to settle for a stable where common animals were kept. I can find no evidence in scripture that supports this.

The Greek word used in Luke 2:7 for "inn" is kataluma, which is the same Greek word translated as "guestchamber" in Mark 14:14 and Luke 22:11. There was no guestchamber available due to the many people that had traveled to Bethlehem for the same reason Joseph and Mary did.

According to the Torah (first five books of Moses) a woman with a blood issue was ritually unclean, she was separated from the rest of the family so as not to defile them. During childbirth and with the issue of blood loss, the same rule applied to women giving birth. With this understanding, there being *"no place for them in the kataluma"* would be completely appropriate for Mary and Joseph not to be able to stay in the house with others of their family or friends.

> Speak unto the children of Israel, saying, If a woman have conceived seed, and born a man child: then she shall be unclean seven days; according to the days of the separation for her infirmity shall she be unclean.
>
> (Leviticus 12:2)

The perfect place for Jesus to be born was in shepherd's field where the sacrificial lambs were birth, Migdal Edar, "Tower of the flock". I believe Jesus was born in the very birthplace where thousands of sacrificial lambs had been born to prefigure Him. John the Baptist said in John 1:29 "Behold the Lamb of God", talking about Jesus. Jesus was not born, as we often picture, behind an inn in a stable where the donkeys of travelers and other animals were left, this is what I believe, yes my traditional thinking is changing to what I believe the Bible reveals. I can't imagine Mary giving birth in such a place where people would be coming and going, possibly hanging out and would be wondering what was going on.

No, I believe God arranges His plans to perfection. The shepherds were the first visitors that God wanted to visit the Christ child; after all they would understand "the Lamb of God" being born where the temple lambs for sacrifice were birth. They were the shepherds that certified the temple lambs for sacrifice.

The sign the angel gave the shepherds was "Ye shall find the babe wrapped in swaddling clothes, lying in the manger". The shepherds knew exactly where to go to find the child; for there was no other manger for the shepherds to consider except the birthing place of the lambs destined for the sacrifice in the temple. They knew exactly where to go by the signs the angels gave them.

> For unto you is born this day in the city of David a Saviour, which is Christ the Lord.
> And this shall be a sign unto you; Ye shall find the babe wrapped in swaddling clothes, lying in a_(Greek interlinear Bible has THE not a) manger.
> (Luke 2:11-12; my emphasis)

The phrase "swaddling clothes" is a translation of the root Greek word SPARGANOO. The word appears in only two verses in the New Testament and both times they appear in Luke 2. The first appearance of SPARGANOO occurs in verse seven and the second is in verse twelve.

The Greek word SPARGANOO is never translated as "burial clothes" and never refers to a burial cloth in the New Testament as some people think.

σπαργανοω <G4683>, σπαργανω: 1 aorist εσπαργανωσα; perfect passive participle εσπαργανωμενος: (σπραγανον a swathing band); "to wrap in swaddling-clothes": an infant just born, Luke 2:7,12. (Ezekiel 16:4; (Euripides, Aristotle), Hippocrates, Plutarch, others.)*

Thayer's *Greek-English Lexicon*

Different Greek words described Jesus' burial process. In Matthew 27:59 we are told that Jesus was wrapped in clean linen cloth. The Greek word for "*wrapped*" is ENTULISSO which was used to describe wrapping a cadaver.

[4] The Greek word that is translated as "linen cloths" in the verse is SINDON. It means "linen cloth of good quality."[5] The same two Greek words, ENTULISSO and SINDON, are used in Luke 23:50 to describe the burial process of Jesus.

> But when the fullness of the time was come, God sent forth his Son, made of a woman, made under the law,
>
> To redeem them that were under the law, that we might receive the adoption of sons.
>
> (Galatians 4:4-5)

> And the angel said unto them, Fear not: for, behold, I bring you good tidings of great joy, which shall be to all people.
>
> For unto you is born this day in the city of David a Saviour, which is Christ the Lord.
>
> And this *shall be* a sign unto you; Ye shall find the babe wrapped in swaddling clothes, lying in a (*the*) manger.
>
> (Luke 2:10-12)

The angels only told the shepherds they would find the Babe wrapped in "swaddling cloths and lying in *the* manger." To these shepherds the sign of ***the*** manger could mean only their manger at the tower of the flock.

THE STAR

> The heavens declare the glory of God; and the firmament sheweth his handywork.
>
> Day unto day uttereth speech, and night unto night sheweth knowledge.
>
> *There is* no speech nor language, *where* their voice is not heard.
>
> Their line is gone out through all the earth, and their words to the end of the world. In them hath he set a tabernacle for the sun,
>
> (Psalm 19:1-4)

Let us look at some of the astrological and biblical factors that may have brought the wise men to Jerusalem. The New Testament says the wise men saw the "star *"rising* in the east, it would most naturally be called a "morning star."

> Now when Jesus was born in Bethlehem of Judaea in the days of Herod the king, behold, there came wise men from the east to Jerusalem,
> Saying, Where is he that is born King of the Jews? For we have seen <u>his star</u> in the east, and are come to worship him.
>
> (Matthew 2:1-2)

> I Jesus have sent mine angel to testify unto you these things in the churches. I am the root and the offspring of David, *and* the bright and morning star.
>
> (Revelation 22:16)

> We have also a more sure word of prophecy; whereunto ye do well that ye take heed, as unto a light that shineth in a dark place, until the day dawn, and the day star arise in your hearts:
>
> (2 Peter 1:19)

Many have tried to explain the star, was it a supernova or a comet, was it a conjunction of several celestial bodies? Some people also think that the star might have been especially created by God, to guide the wise men and that there isn't a scientific explanation. The Greek word translated "star" really means "radiance." The "star" could therefore have been what the Jews called the "Shekinah" — that is, a physical manifestation of the glory of God in the form of a supernatural radiance. The Hebrews experienced this in the wilderness of Sinai as God led them out of Egypt by a pillar of cloud in the day and a pillar of fire by night.

The word Shekinah is from the Hebrew word "shekinot" which means to "settle in" or "dwell with." or where God's Divine Presence dwells. The Shekinah glory filled the tabernacle in the wilderness, and led the Hebrews while traveling in the wilderness, where God was a light at night and a cloud by day, and also filled the temple in Jerusalem.

> And the LORD went before them by day in a pillar of a cloud, to lead them the way; and by night in a pillar of fire, to give them light; to go by day and night:
>
> (Exodus 13:21)

> Now when Solomon had made an end of praying, the fire came down from heaven, and consumed the burnt offering and the sacrifices; and the glory of the LORD filled the house.
>
> (2 Chronicles 7:1)

In the book of Ezekiel we find that God removed the Shekinah Glory from the Temple before it was destroyed. The Shekinah Glory is mentioned in the New Testament as being present:

- At the birth of Jesus
  And, lo, the angel of the Lord came upon them, and the glory of the Lord shone round about them: and they were sore afraid.
  (Luke 2:9)

- At His transfiguration
  While he yet spake, behold, a bright cloud overshadowed them: and behold a voice out of the cloud, which said, This is my beloved Son, in whom I am well pleased; hear ye him.
  (Matthew 17:5)

- At His ascension (Acts 1:9).
  And when he had spoken these things, while they beheld, he was taken up; and a cloud received him out of their sight.
  (Acts 1:9)

Could the wise men have been guided by the Shekinah glory of God? It will remain a mystery for us how God's creations in the sky played a role in the birth of Jesus and the visit of the wise men.

God's Word says:

> Then God said, "Let there be lights in the firmament of the
> heavens to divide the day from the night; and let them be
> for <u>signs</u> and <u>seasons</u>, and for days and years
>
> (Genesis 1:14)

> Which alone spreadeth out the heavens, and treadeth
> upon the waves of the sea.
>   Which maketh Arcturus, Orion, and Pleiades, and the
> chambers of the south.
>
> (Job 9:8-9)

> Canst thou bind the sweet influences of Pleiades, or loose
> the bands of Orion?
>   Canst thou bring forth Mazzaroth in his season? or
> canst thou guide Arcturus with his sons?
>   Knowest thou the ordinances of heaven? canst thou
> set the dominion thereof in the earth?
>
> (Job 38:31-33)

Whatever the star was it was a creation by God for the wise men to follow
and find the child Jesus with His mother living in a house.

THE WISE MEN

> Now when Jesus was born in Bethlehem of Judaea in the
> days of Herod the king, behold, there came wise men from
> the east to Jerusalem...
>
> (Matthew 2:1)

Who were these Wise Men and from where did they come? Another name
for wise men was Magi.

The only true facts we have about these particular magi are given in the
first twelve verses of Matthew chapter 2. We are not told how many there
were, their names, or their means of transportation or the countries from

which they came. The fact that they came from the east would lead us to believe they came from the Persia, Babylon area.

> In the third year of the reign of Jehoiakim king of Judah came Nebuchadnezzar king of Babylon unto Jerusalem, and besieged it.
>
> And the Lord gave Jehoiakim king of Judah into his hand, with part of the vessels of the house of God: which he carried into the land of Shinar to the house of his god; and he brought the vessels into the treasure house of his god.
>
> And the king spake unto Ashpenaz the master of his eunuchs, that he should bring *certain* of the children of Israel, and of the king's seed, and of the princes;
>
> Children in whom *was* no blemish, but well favoured, and skilful in all wisdom, and cunning in knowledge, and understanding science, and such as *had* ability in them to stand in the king's palace, and whom they might teach the learning and the tongue of the Chaldeans.
>
> And the king appointed them a daily provision of the king's meat, and of the wine which he drank: so nourishing them three years, that at the end thereof they might stand before the king.
>
> Now among these were of the children of Judah, Daniel, Hananiah, Mishael, and Azariah:
>
> Unto whom the prince of the eunuchs gave names: for he gave unto Daniel the *name* of Belteshazzar; and to Hananiah, of Shadrach; and to Mishael, of Meshach; and to Azariah, of Abednego.
>
> (Daniel 1:1-7)

When Daniel was taken captive to Babylon he was made the head of the wise men for the king. I'm sure Daniel left a powerful testimony on the men he was in charge of in Babylon and no doubt his testimony was passed down through the generations of magi.

If these wise men were of the Babylonian wise men formerly led by Daniel, that came to visit Jesus, then they were probably aware of Daniel's prophecies, including Daniel's reference to the timing of the coming of the Messiah, see Daniel chapter 9. Daniel no doubt would have introduced them to his God. These wise men were Astronomers.

The ancient Roman historian Philo describes these men this way:

"Among the Persians there is a body of the Magi, who, investigating the works of nature for the purpose of becoming acquainted with the truth, do at their leisure become initiated themselves and initiate others in the divine virtues by very clear explanations."

> Then the king made Daniel a great man, and gave him many great gifts, and made him ruler over the whole province of Babylon, and chief of the governors over all the wise *men* of Babylon.
>
> (Daniel 2:48)

What is the difference between astronomy and astrology?

Astronomy is a science that studies everything outside of the earth's atmosphere, such as planets, stars, asteroids, galaxies; and the properties and relationships of those celestial bodies. Astronomers base their studies on research and observation. These wise men or magi as some call them were Astronomers. They studied the stars they did not worship them.

Here David is telling us the stars communicate giving out messages:

> The heavens declare the glory of God: and the firmament sheweth his handywork.
> Day unto day uttereth speech, and night unto night sheweth knowledge.
> *There is* no speech nor language, *where* their voice is not heard.
> Their line is gone out through all the earth, and their words to the end of the world. In them hath he set a tabernacle for the sun.
>
> (Psalm 19:1-4)

In Romans chapter 10 Paul emphasizes what David said in Psalms:

> So then faith *cometh* by hearing, and hearing by the word
> of God.
> But I say, Have they not heard? Yes verily, their sound
> went into all the earth, and their words unto the ends of
> the world.
>
> (Romans 10:17-18)

> And there shall be signs in the sun, and in the moon, and
> in the stars;
>
> (Luke 21:25)

Astrology includes several groups of traditional systems basically classified as Eastern and Western ones that use the position of the planets and stars at the time of an individual's birth to predict his future, personality, important events of his life etc. fortune tellers, palm readers, horoscopes, witchcraft etc. The Bible forbids this type of activity.

The Old Testament decreed the death penalty for astrology.

Astronomy is a science, and **astrology** is not.

> Now the works of the flesh are manifest, which are *these*;
> Adultery, fornication, uncleanness, lasciviousness,
> Idolatry, witchcraft, hatred, variance, emulations,
> wrath, strife, seditions, heresies,
> Envyings, murders, drunkenness, revellings, and such
> like: of the which I tell you before, as I have also told *you* in
> time past, that they which do such things shall not inherit
> the kingdom of God.
>
> (Galatians 5:19-21)

How many wise men the Bible does not tell us. We assume there were three because of the three gifts, there could have been ten or twelve of the magi. In those days people travelled in caravans for protection against thieves; nor does the Bible not tell us the mode of travel was by camel.

THE THREE GIFTS

1. <u>Gold</u> is a precious metal and is a symbol of divinity. The gift of gold to the Christ child was symbolic of His divinity—God in flesh. A gift for a king.

2. <u>Frankincense</u> is a white resin or gum and is a symbol of holiness and righteousness. The gift of frankincense to the Christ child was symbolic of His willingness to become a sacrifice, wholly giving Himself up. This is also obviously an incense, the burning of which represents prayer. It is used by priests, and indicates the priestly nature of the Messiah.

3. <u>Myrrh</u> is a product of Arabia, and was a spice used in embalming. Myrrh symbolizes bitterness, suffering, and affliction. Jesus would grow to suffer greatly as a man and would pay the ultimate price when He gave His life on the cross for all who would believe in Him. The inclusion of this gift can be seen as prophetic of the death of the Messiah.

The three gifts together are symbolic of the Messiah's offices as prophet, priest and king.

These gifts could have sustained the family when they travelled to Egypt to flee from King Herod.

TIME AND PLACE OF THE VISIT

Now when Jesus was born in Bethlehem of Judaea in the days of Herod the king, behold, there came wise men from the east to Jerusalem,
Saying, Where is he that is born King of the Jews? for we have seen his star in the east, and are come to worship him.

When Herod the king had heard *these things*, he was troubled, and all Jerusalem with him.

And when he had gathered all the chief priests and scribes of the people together, he demanded of them where Christ should be born.

And they said unto him, In Bethlehem of Judaea: for thus it is written by the prophet,

And thou Bethlehem, *in* the land of Juda, art not the least among the princes of Juda: for out of thee shall come a Governor, that shall rule my people Israel.

Then Herod, when he had privily called the wise men, enquired of them diligently what time the star appeared.

And he sent them to Bethlehem, and said, Go and search diligently for the young child; and when ye have found *him*, bring me word again, that I may come and worship him also.

(Matthew 2:1-8)

So Herod sent the wise men to Bethlehem and from the Book of Matthew we learn:

- Jesus was born during the days of Herod the king.
- Wise men from the East came searching for this "King of the Jews".
- Chief priests and scribes revealed to Herod the birth place of this "King of the Jews"
- Then Herod sent the wise men to Bethlehem to search for the babe.

When they had heard the king, they departed; and, lo, the star, which they saw in the east, went before them, till it came and stood over where the young child was.

When they saw the star, they rejoiced with exceeding great joy.

And when they were come into the house, they saw the young child with Mary his mother, and fell down, and worshipped him: and when they had opened their treasures, they presented unto him gifts; gold, and frankincense, and myrrh.

And being warned of God in a dream that they should not return to Herod, they departed into their own country another way.

(Matthew 2:9-12)

Matthew does not say that the wise men headed for Bethlehem, but that they followed the star till it came and stood over where the young child was. (He was no longer a babe but a young child).

In the original Greek texts, of Luke's gospel that records the birth of Jesus, the shepherds were seeing a "brephos," which means newborn baby, or infant; but in Matthew, it's a different Greek word. It is "paidion," and means young child, and is never translated in your Bible as babe or baby or infant or newborn. There is a difference in the time frame of Matthew and Luke concerning Jesus age. The wise men did not visit Jesus in the manger as did the shepherds. In Matthew when the wise men saw Jesus he was a young child and in Luke He was a babe just born.

Now let us go back to the Gospel of Luke chapter 2 which gives us more detail on the birth and activity of Joseph and Mary after the birth.

And when eight days were accomplished for the circumcising of the child, his name was called JESUS, which was so named of the angel before he was conceived in the womb.

(Luke 2:21)

And in the eighth day the flesh of his foreskin shall be circumcised.

(Leviticus 12:3)

As was the law, Jesus was circumcised <u>on the eighth day,</u> (eight days old here) in Bethlehem. I believe the family stayed in Bethlehem until the purification of Mary, after her purification they returned to Nazareth. This is my belief the Bible does not say how long they stayed in Bethlehem after the birth of Jesus, but it does say after her purification they returned to Nazareth. I believe this is the first time they went back to Nazareth after the birth. The distance from Nazareth to Jerusalem is about around ninety miles and Bethlehem to Jerusalem is about five miles.

Chapter 3

AT THE TEMPLE

And the LORD spake unto Moses, saying,

Speak unto the children of Israel, saying, If a woman have conceived seed, and born a man child: then she shall be unclean seven days; according to the days of the separation for her infirmity shall she be unclean.

And in the eighth day the flesh of his foreskin shall be circumcised.

And she shall then continue in the blood of her purifying three and thirty days; she shall touch no hallowed thing, nor come into the sanctuary, until the days of her purifying be fulfilled.

(Leviticus 12:1-4)

And when the days of her purification according to the law of Moses were accomplished, they brought him to Jerusalem, to present *him* to the Lord;

(As it is written in the law of the Lord, Every male that openeth the womb shall be called holy to the Lord;)

And to offer a sacrifice according to that which is said in the law of the Lord, A pair of turtledoves, or two young pigeons.

(Luke 2:22-24)

And when they had performed all things according to the law of the Lord, they returned into Galilee, to their own city Nazareth.

(Luke 2:39)

I believe Jesus was 40 days old when they left Jerusalem and returned to their home in Nazareth.

Mary was unclean after the birth for seven days	days 7
Visits the temple and Jesus is circumcised on the eighth day	
Jesus presented at the temple and Mary's purification	<u>days 33</u>
TOTAL	days 40

Now turn back to the scripture in Matthew when the wise men seen Jesus he was a young child not a babe in the manger. Matthew does not say that the wise men headed for Bethlehem, but that they followed the star till it came and stood over where the young child was. (He was no longer a babe but a young child). I believe the wise men were lead to the home of Joseph and Mary in Nazareth; after Jesus was presented in the temple and after Mary's purification, they had returned to Nazareth, their own city.

The three gifts were symbolic of Jesus and perhaps they also provided a way to travel to Egypt as I stated earlier. We do not know the value of these gifts just that they were valuable.

The wise men worshipped Jesus and obeyed God by returning to their own country another way, they did not go back to Jerusalem to Herod.

FLIGHT INTO EGYPT

After the visit of the wise men God appeared in a dream to Joseph and told him to flee to Egypt.

God is warning Joseph of the plans of Herod to kill all the children in Bethlehem. Herod was a Roman appointed-king of Judea about 37-4 BC in Jerusalem. He was a ruthless man who did not hesitate to kill anyone who was a threat to his throne.

And when they were departed, behold, the angel of the
Lord appeareth to Joseph in a dream, saying, Arise, and
take the young child and his mother, and flee into Egypt,
and be thou there until I bring thee word: for Herod will
seek the young child to destroy him.

When he arose, he took the young child and his
mother by night, and departed into Egypt:

And was there until the death of Herod: that it might
be fulfilled which was spoken of the Lord by the prophet,
saying, Out of Egypt have I called my son.

Then Herod, when he saw that he was mocked of the
wise men, was exceeding wroth, and sent forth, and slew
all the children that were in Bethlehem, and in all the
coasts thereof, from two years old and under, according to
the time which he had diligently enquired of the wise men.

(Matthew 2:13-16)

The Bible does not give the exact age of Jesus at the time they fled to Egypt.
All the information we have is in Matthew 2:13-16 which states that they
fled after the wise men departed and after the angel appeared to Joseph.
They left immediately during the night and the family stayed in Egypt until
after the death of Herod. How long they stayed in Egypt the Bible does not
tell us, but after the death of Herod, an angel appears again to Joseph in a
dream and tells him that Herod is dead who sought to kill Jesus.

But when Herod was dead, behold, an angel of the Lord
appeareth in a dream to Joseph in Egypt,

Saying, Arise, and take the young child and his
mother, and go into the land of Israel: for they are dead
which sought the young child's life.

And he arose, and took the young child and his
mother, and came into the land of Israel.

(Matthew 2:19-21)

According to Ernest Martin, there were four total lunar eclipses visible in Judea

1. March 23, 5 BC
2. September 15, 5 BC

3. March 13, 4 BC
4. January 10, 1 BC

Herod died in the interval Josephus mentioned that occurred between a lunar eclipse and a Passover, however it wasn't 4 BC or 5 BC. Dr. Martin, along with other historians of that time has given us the same details as Josephus, proving King Herod could NOT HAVE DIED before the first three dates given above and completed the events of his funeral in three weeks.

Dr. Martin has carefully scrutinized the account of Josephus, the succession of rulers, the lunar eclipse that was used to establish that date and has come to demonstrate an overwhelming hypothesis that Herod died in mid-January 1 BC.

> ASKELM.com/star, *The Star of Bethlehem* by Dr. Ernest Martin, chapter 8

The Young Child-Years of Silence

Little is recorded in scripture concerning the life of Jesus from the time of the family's return to Nazareth from Egypt. The largest part of Jesus life is not known, but the Bible says He grew and waxed strong in the spirit, filled with wisdom and the grace of God. We have through His birth to around 2 years, then He returns in the temple at the age of 12. His silent years he spend in Nazareth growing up as any other young Jewish child and learning his earthly father, Joseph's trade as carpenter during his teenage years. Jesus is referred to in one place as "is this not the carpenter"? Mary and Joseph also had other children, so Jesus did have half-brothers and sisters.

> Is not this the carpenter, the son of Mary, the brother of James, and Joses, and of Juda, and Simon? and are not his sisters here with us? And they were offended at him.
>
> (Mark 6:3)

When Mark wrote this scripture, "Is not this the carpenter, the son of Mary..." no doubt Joseph had died and the family consisted of only Mary and the half-brothers and sisters of Jesus. Joseph is last mentioned when Jesus was twelve and traveled to the Temple for the feast of Passover. I believe Joseph had died before Jesus started His ministry. The Bible does not say other than there is no mention of Joseph.

> And when they had performed all things according to the law of the Lord, they returned into Galilee, to their own city Nazareth.
> And the child grew, and waxed strong in spirit, filled with wisdom: and the grace of God was upon him.
>
> (Luke 2:39-40)

A YOUNG BOY IN THE TEMPLE

> Now his parents went to Jerusalem every year at the feast of the Passover.
> And when he was twelve years old, they went up to Jerusalem after the custom of the feast.
> And when they had fulfilled the days, as they returned, the child Jesus tarried behind in Jerusalem; and Joseph and his mother knew not of it.
>
> (Luke 2:41-43)

Now when Joseph and Mary realized Jesus was not with them, they returned to Jerusalem and searched for Him. Mary reprimanded Jesus when they found Him in the temple sitting with the doctors and teachers listening to them and asking questions.

> And when they found him not, they turned back again to Jerusalem, seeking him.
> And it came to pass, that after three days they found him in the temple, sitting in the midst of the doctors, both hearing them, and asking them questions.
> And all that heard him were astonished at his understanding and answers.

> And when they saw him, they were amazed: and his
> mother said unto him, Son, why hast thou thus dealt with
> us? behold, **thy father** and I have sought thee sorrowing.
> And he said unto them, How is it that ye sought me?
> wist ye not that I must be about **my Father's** business?
> (Luke 2:45-49)

Jesus amazed the teachers in the temple and His earthly parents with His understanding and His answers

Mary says...... thy father referring to Joseph

Jesus says...... My Father's referring to God

The answer Jesus gave to his mother may have seemed a bit rude to some of us, but it was not, according the Jewish culture. Jesus knew God's plan for His life and God's plan was revealed to Mary and Joseph a portion at a time. I believe Mary and Joseph knew Jesus was the Son of God and was to save His people, but as to the exact plan of God, I believe it was revealed little at a time. I don't believe Joseph and Mary knew the Jesus would give His life to save the people at this time.

> And they understood not the saying which he spake unto
> them.
> And he went down with them, and came to Nazareth,
> and was subject unto them: but his mother kept all these
> sayings in her heart.
> And Jesus increased in wisdom and stature, and in
> favour with God and man.
> (Luke 2:50-52)

Jesus revealed to His parents, He knew God was his Father. They knew Jesus was the Son of God and about His divine nature and His conception was from God by the Holy Spirit and why He came into the world. They did not know the full plan of God for the life of Jesus, that He would give His life and rise again and return to heaven.

How do you raise a son whom you believe to be your saviour, the Son of God? Mary's own son calls God his Father. How can Mary understand and take all this in? From the time the angel, Gabriel appeared to Mary, her visit with Elizabeth, the shepherds' visit, Simeon's and Anna's words of blessing in the temple when He was taken to the temple; all these things Mary has been <u>pondering</u> in her heart and now this incident in the temple at the age of twelve. He was so knowledgeable beyond His age of the things of God.

Pondered. Weighed. This is the original meaning of the word weighed. She kept them; she revolved them; she weighed them in her mind, giving to each circumstance its just importance, and anxiously seeking what it might indicate respecting her child.

Barnes' Notes on the New Testament.

I quote Alfred Edersheim, "Had Mary known the complete mission from the beginning—that He was fully God and fully man—the human side could never have been fulfilled. The thought of His divinity would have been too all-consuming. What bond could His family or disciples have shared with Him if they had known they spoke with God? Christ humbled Himself to live as we do (Hebrews 4:15), something that would have been impossible if all had been known from the beginning".

"Beyond this, the gradual revelation of Jesus's mission also provided important instruction to those closest to Him. Just as the disciples came to understand whom they followed, Mary realized day by day, revelation by revelation, that she had indeed given birth to the Son of the living God. The lessons had all the greater impact being understood gradually than they would have if given all at once".

Edersheim, Alfred. *The Life and Times of Jesus the Messiah.* Hendrickson Publishers, 1993.

Jesus returns to Nazareth with His earthly parents and continued in subjection to them.

Jesus was not an ordinary child, He was born of a virgin, and He was God in human flesh and had come to do the will of His Father, but His early years were no doubt spent as any young child growing up in the Galilee area.

> And the child grew, and waxed strong in spirit, filled with wisdom: and the grace of God was upon him.
>
> (Luke 2:40)

Chapter 4

MINISTRY OF JESUS AS THE SERVANT

If Jesus was God in the flesh why does He need to grow in wisdom? Doesn't God know everything?

Made himself of no reputation— Greek, **εαυτον εκενωσε**, literally, *he emptied himself;* (Jesus lay down his divine nature)

> Let this mind be in you, which was also in Christ Jesus:
>> Who, being in the form of God, thought it not robbery to be equal with God:
>> But made himself of no reputation, and took upon him the form of a servant, and was made in the likeness of men:
>>> (Philippians 2:5-7)

The incarnation means that while Jesus was God, He took upon a new nature – a human nature. Jesus was fully God and fully human, He laid aside His divine nature and became man. To see God is to see Jesus. Jesus once said "My Father and I are one".

No man hath seen God at any time; the only begotten Son, which is in the bosom of the Father, he hath declared him.

(John 1:18)

Then answered Jesus and said unto them, Verily, verily, I say unto you, The Son can do nothing of himself, but what he seeth the Father do: for what things soever he doeth, these also doeth the Son likewise.

For the Father loveth the Son, and sheweth him all things that himself doeth: and he will shew him greater works than these, that ye may marvel.

(John 5:19-20)

Philip saith unto him, Lord, shew us the Father, and it sufficeth us.

Jesus saith unto him, Have I been so long time with you, and yet hast thou not known me, Philip? He that hath seen me hath seen the Father; and how sayest thou then, Shew us the Father?

(John 14:8-9)

Now I say that Jesus Christ was a minister of the circumcision for the truth of God, to confirm the promises made unto the fathers:

And that the Gentiles might glorify God for his mercy; as it is written, For this cause I will confess to thee among the Gentiles, and sing unto thy name.

(Romans 15:8-9)

Even as the Son of man came not to be ministered unto, but to minister, and to give his life a ransom for many.

(Matthew 20:28)

Jesus did not come into the world to be served, but to serve, and to give His life as a ransom for many.

JESUS IS BAPTIZED

Now there in the Jordan Valley a man dressed in camel's hair was baptizing those who had come with repentance of heart. John the Baptist was not an ordinary man, but a special man set apart by God to prepare the way for the Messiah. There had been 400 years of silence since the last Old Testament prophet, Malachi. John was called the last of the Old Testament prophets linking the Old Testament with the New Testament; his preaching was the end of the Law and the beginning of the Promise. The children of Israel lived according to the Laws that God gave to Moses, now a new message was being preached, John's ministry and preaching was a change in direction than that of the Old Testament. John the Baptist came proclaiming the Kingdom of God. Then one day as the crowds begin to thin came Jesus to be baptized of John.

> Now in the fifteenth year of the reign of Tiberius Caesar, Pontius Pilate being governor of Judaea, and Herod being tetrarch of Galilee, and his brother Philip tetrarch of Ituraea and of the region of Trachonitis, and Lysanias the tetrarch of Abilene,
>
> Annas and Caiaphas being the high priests, the word of God came unto John the son of Zacharias in the wilderness.
>
> And he came into all the country about Jordan, preaching the baptism of repentance for the remission of sins;
>
> (Luke 3:1-3)

> Now when all the people were baptized, it came to pass, that Jesus also being baptized, and praying, the heaven was opened,
>
> And the Holy Ghost descended in a bodily shape like a dove upon him, and a voice came from heaven, which said, Thou art my beloved Son; in thee I am well pleased.
>
> And Jesus himself began to be about thirty years of age, being (as was supposed) the son of Joseph, which was the son of Heli,
>
> (Luke 3:21-23)

And it came to pass in those days, that Jesus came from Nazareth of Galilee, and was baptized of John in Jordan.

And straightway coming up out of the water, he saw the heavens opened, and the Spirit like a dove descending upon him:

And there came a voice from heaven, saying, Thou art my beloved Son, in whom I am well pleased.

And immediately the Spirit driveth him into the wilderness.

And he was there in the wilderness forty days, tempted of Satan; and was with the wild beasts; and the angels ministered unto him.

(Mark 1:9-13)

The next day John seeth Jesus coming unto him, and saith, Behold the Lamb of God, which taketh away the sin of the world.

This is he of whom I said, After me cometh a man which is preferred before me: for he was before me.

And I knew him not: but that he should be made manifest to Israel, therefore am I come baptizing with water.

And John bare record, saying, I saw the Spirit descending from heaven like a dove, and it abode upon him.

And I knew him not: but he that sent me to baptize with water, the same said unto me, Upon whom thou shalt see the Spirit descending, and remaining on him, the same is he which baptizeth with the Holy Ghost.

And I saw, and bare record that this is the Son of God.

(John 1:29-34)

Jesus was baptized by John the Baptist in the River of Jordan to fulfill all righteousness. He who had no sin took His place among those who had no righteousness. He who was without sin submitted to a baptism for sinners.

The Baptism of Jesus marks the inauguration of Jesus' earthly ministry as well as marking the beginning of the decline of John the Baptist's ministry.

Many in Israel wondered if John might be the Messiah. Yet the last prophet declares with assurance that he is not even worthy to untie the laces of the Messiah's sandals (Matthew 3:11). John, the official herald of the coming king was waiting for Christ to be revealed. The baptism of Jesus fulfills that need as the Messiah is identified to John by God

> And I knew him not: but he that sent me to baptize with water, the same said unto me, Upon whom thou shalt see the Spirit descending, and remaining on him, the same is he which baptizeth with the Holy Ghost.
> And I saw, and bare record that this is the Son of God.
> (John 1:33-34)

At his baptism the death, burial and resurrection of Jesus is first prefigured. It is here at his baptism that the perfect one identifies himself with sinners, and demonstrates his full humility. His baptism is where the redemptive ministry of Jesus Christ begins.

> In the beginning was the Word, and the Word was with God, and the Word was God.
> The same was in the beginning with God.
> All things were made by him; and without him was not any thing made that was made.
> In him was life; and the life was the light of men.
> And the light shineth in darkness; and the darkness comprehended it not.
> There was a man sent from God, whose name was John.
> The same came for a witness, to bear witness of the Light, that all men through him might believe.
> (John 1:1-7)

John's purpose in coming with a baptism of water was to reveal the Lamb of God to Israel. John's baptism was done with water calling for the repentance of sin, and also for Christ to be revealed, to mark the beginning of His ministry. In this way righteousness was being fulfilled.

For he hath made him to be sin for us, who knew no sin;
that we might be made the righteousness of God in him.

(2 Corinthians 5:21)

- Jesus' being baptized was an act of identification.
- Jesus was associating himself with us.
- He took the place of a sinner, and was baptized with a baptism of repentance and confession of sin even though He had never sinned. He took our sins.
- Jesus' coming to John showed His approval of John's baptism, bearing witness to it, that it was from heaven and approved by God.

I also believe the baptism of Jesus was a ceremonial anointing; in the Old Testament the priest hood was of the Levitical order and must be of priestly descent, a direct descendant (following the male line) of Aaron, the brother of Moses. The succession was to be father to son and remain in Aaron's family. After the return from the Babylon Exile the succession continued father to son for a while, then later become appointed by the Roman authorities. This was going against God's instructions and leading to a corrupt priesthood.

John the Baptist was the son of Zacharias, a priest in the lineage of Aaron. Both John's parents were descent from Aaron from the tribe of Levi. Zacharias was of the course of Abia (the 8th course). So this puts John the Baptist in the priestly line being the son of a priest. John the Baptist was the forerunner of Jesus, to call the people of Israel to righteousness and to pass the priesthood to Jesus, the High Priest after the Order of Melchizedek.

I want to inject here some information about Melchizedek. We read about this man in the book of Genesis and again in Hebrews. He was a priest and king, he was not of the Levitical priests, his office was different from theirs and Jesus priesthood was to resemble his. Jesus was not only to be our priest but He is our High Priest and our King.

Jesus became high priest forever according to the order of Melchizedeck.
BUT, WHAT DOES THIS MEAN?
It means that Christ was not a High Priest, as in Aaron and the Levitical order (according to the Law of Moses). The High Priesthood of Jesus Christ -- the

writer is affirming a higher order! Christ was and is a High Priest like Melchizedek; not like Aaron or Levi. Note the following:

1. *Melchizedek's position as High Priest was not dependent on ancestry... neither was Christ's. (7:14).*

2. *Melchizedek was not in a succession of many priests... neither is Christ. (7:3).*

3. *Melchizedek's priesthood was higher than and separate from the Levitical order... so is Christ's. (7:4-7).*

4. *Melchizedek was priest and king... so is Christ! (See Zech. 6:9-15).*

5. *Melchizedek received tribute from Abraham, the father of the Jewish nation; this shows the superiority of Melchizedek's priesthood above the Levitical (which came out of the loins of Abraham). {See Gen. 14:18-20 with Heb. 7:4}."*

Steven Rudd steve.rudd@bible.ca by Warren E. Berkley

And Melchizedek king of Salem brought forth bread and wine: and he was the priest of the most high God.

And he blessed him, and said, Blessed be Abram of the most high God, possessor of heaven and earth:

And blessed be the most high God, which hath delivered thine enemies into thy hand. And he gave him tithes of all.

(Genesis 14:18-20)

And no man taketh this honour unto himself, but he that is called of God, as was Aaron.

So also Christ glorified not himself to be made an high priest; but he that said unto him, Thou art my Son, to day have I begotten thee.

As he saith also in another place, Thou art a priest for ever after the order of Melchisedec.

(Hebrews 5:4-6)

For this Melchisedec, king of Salem, priest of the most high God, who met Abraham returning from the slaughter of the kings, and blessed him;

To whom also Abraham gave a tenth part of all; first being by interpretation King of righteousness, and after that also King of Salem, which is, King of peace;

Without father, without mother, without descent, having neither beginning of days, nor end of life; but made like unto the Son of God; abideth a priest continually.

(Hebrews 7:1-3)

And Moses brought Aaron and his sons, and washed them with water.

(Leviticus 8:6)

I also believe that the baptism of Jesus was symbolic of the priestly anointing. John the Baptist representing the Levitical priesthood (remember John was the son of a Levitical priest, Zacharias) transferred his office to Jesus the new high priest after the Order of Melchizekek.

The heavens opened revealing Jesus as the Son of God and the dove resting upon Jesus represented the anointing of the Holy Spirit. John's ministry was about to end, and Jesus' role as high priest of the Order of Melchizedek, the eternal order was superseding the Levitical Order of the Old Covenant. God changes the priesthood from the tribe of Levi to the tribe of Judah.

Jesus ordination was not a religious ceremony, but God's proclamation at His baptism, *"This is my beloved Son in whom I am well-pleased"* as the Holy Spirit descended in the form of a dove and anointed Him. Remember the priests were anointed with oil in the Old Testament. A dove is symbolic of the Holy Spirit and oil.

Oil was involved in the anointing of the prophets, priests and kings for ministry to their offices. Oil symbolizes the soothing and healing presence of the Holy Spirit.

That word, I say, ye know, which was published throughout all Judaea, and began from Galilee, after the baptism which John preached;

How God anointed Jesus of Nazareth with the Holy Ghost and with power: who went about doing good, and healing all that were oppressed of the devil; for God was with him.

(Acts 10:37-38)

Without father, without mother, without descent, having neither beginning of days, nor end of life; but made like unto the Son of God; abideth a priest continually.

(Hebrews 7:3)

For every high priest taken from among men is ordained for men in things pertaining to God, that he may offer both gifts and sacrifices for sins:

Who can have compassion on the ignorant, and on them that are out of the way; for that he himself also is compassed with infirmity.

And by reason hereof he ought, as for the people, so also for himself, to offer for sins.

And no man taketh this honour unto himself, but he that is called of God, as was Aaron.

So also <u>Christ glorified not himself to be made an high priest; but he that said unto him, Thou art my Son, to day have I begotten thee.</u>

As he saith also in another place, Thou art a priest for ever after the order of Melchisedec.

(Hebrews 5:1-6)

If therefore perfection were by the Levitical priesthood, (for under it the people received the law,) what further need was there that another priest should rise after the order of Melchisedec, and not be called after the order of Aaron?

For the priesthood being changed, there is made of necessity a change also of the law.

For he of whom these things are spoken pertaineth to another tribe, of which no man gave attendance at the altar.

For it is evident that our Lord sprang out of Juda; of which tribe Moses spake nothing concerning priesthood.

And it is yet far more evident: for that after the similitude of Melchisedec there ariseth another priest,

Who is made, not after the law of a carnal commandment, but after the power of an endless life.

For he testifieth, Thou art a priest for ever after the order of Melchisedec.

For there is verily a disannulling of the commandment going before for the weakness and unprofitableness thereof.

For the law made nothing perfect, but the bringing in of a better hope did; by the which we draw nigh unto God.

And inasmuch as not without an oath he was made priest:

(For those priests were made without an oath; but this with an oath by him that said unto him, The Lord sware and will not repent, Thou art a priest for ever after the order of Melchisedec:)

By so much was Jesus made a surety of a better testament.

And they truly were many priests, because they were not suffered to continue by reason of death:

But this man, because he continueth ever, hath an unchangeable priesthood.

Wherefore he is able also to save them to the uttermost that come unto God by him, seeing he ever liveth to make intercession for them.

For such an high priest became us, who is holy, harmless, undefiled, separate from sinners, and made higher than the heavens;

Who needeth not daily, as those high priests, to offer up sacrifice, first for his own sins, and then for the people's: for this he did once, when he offered up himself.

> For the law maketh men high priests which have infirmity; but the word of the oath, which was since the law, maketh the Son, who is consecrated for evermore.
>
> (Hebrews 7:11-28)

Jesus priesthood far exceeded that of the Levitical Order. Jesus Christ instituted a new priestly order, not of a few select individuals, but of all those who are born again. Jesus is our high priest and we, if cleansed by the blood of Jesus Christ and believers are of His royal priesthood.

> But ye are a chosen generation, a royal priesthood, an holy nation, a peculiar people; that ye should shew forth the praises of him who hath called you out of darkness into his marvellous light:
>
> (1 Peter 2:9)

Jesus came to John before He began His ministry to be baptized of him.

> Then cometh Jesus from Galilee to Jordan unto John, to be baptized of him.
>
> But John forbad him, saying, I have need to be baptized of thee, and comest thou to me?
>
> And Jesus answering said unto him, Suffer it to be so now: for thus it becometh us to fulfil all righteousness. Then he suffered him.
>
> (Matthew 3:13-15)

Was Jesus baptized on Yom Kippur (Day of Atonement)?

The Bible does not tell us the day Jesus was baptized, however it is interesting to note that what the high priest did on Yom Kippur seems to foretell what happened to Jesus at the time of His baptism. Let us look at Yom Kippur and see what the Bible says, what was this special day, what did the children of Israel do on this day in the Old Testament.

Yom Kippur (Day of Atonement) is probably the most important holiday of the Jewish year. Many Jews who do not observe any other Jewish custom will fast, refrain from work and attend synagogue services on this day.

Yom Kippur occurs on the tenth day of Tishri. The holiday is instituted at Leviticus 23:26

> And the LORD spake unto Moses, saying,
>
> Also on the tenth day of this seventh month there shall be a day of atonement: it shall be an holy convocation unto you; and ye shall afflict your souls, and offer an offering made by fire unto the LORD.
>
> And ye shall do no work in that same day: for it is a day of atonement, to make an atonement for you before the LORD your God.
>
> For whatsoever soul it be that shall not be afflicted in that same day, he shall be cut off from among his people.
>
> And whatsoever soul it be that doeth any work in that same day, the same soul will I destroy from among his people.
>
> Ye shall do no manner of work: it shall be a statute for ever throughout your generations in all your dwellings.
>
> It shall be unto you a sabbath of rest, and ye shall afflict your souls: in the ninth day of the month at even, from even unto even, shall ye celebrate your sabbath.
>
> (Leviticus 23:26-32)

> And he shall take the two goats, and present them before the LORD at the door of the tabernacle of the congregation.
>
> And Aaron shall cast lots upon the two goats; one lot for the LORD, and the other lot for the scapegoat.
>
> And Aaron shall bring the goat upon which the LORD'S lot fell, and offer him for a sin offering.
>
> But the goat, on which the lot fell to be the scapegoat, shall be presented alive before the LORD, to make an atonement with him, and to let him go for a scapegoat into the wilderness.
>
> (Leviticus 16:7-10)

On the Day of Atonement the High Priest would wash himself, put on his priestly garments and proceed to his duties, offering one goat as a sin offering for all Israel, then the other goat by putting his hands upon his head and placing all the sins of Israel on it, the goat was led out into the wilderness as a scapegoat.

> And Jesus being full of the Holy Ghost returned from Jordan, and was led by the Spirit into the wilderness,
> (Luke 4:1)

Jesus was indeed the Lamb of God that was sacrificed for our sins as we will discuss later. Was the Day of Atonement a foreshadowing of the activities that took place when Jesus was baptized in the Jordan River?

Baptism is a public declaration that you have accepted Christ as your savior and desire to follow in His footsteps. Baptism speaks primarily of a personal, public identification with Jesus Christ; baptism's very purpose is to reveal identity with Jesus.

Some people think John the Baptist did not know who Jesus was even though they were cousins. I don't know for sure but I do believe when Jesus was baptized by John and God spoke and the Holy Spirit descended; this was confirmation to John that Jesus was indeed the son of God and the Messiah. I believe John and Jesus knew each other and that they were cousins, however God's voice and the Holy Spirit's descent at Jesus' baptism was a sign to confirm to John that Jesus was the Messiah.

> The next day John seeth Jesus coming unto him, and saith, Behold the Lamb of God, which taketh away the sin of the world.
> This is he of whom I said, After me cometh a man which is preferred before me: for he was before me.
> And I knew him not: but that he should be made manifest to Israel, therefore am I come baptizing with water.
> And John bare record, saying, I saw the Spirit descending from heaven like a dove, and it abode upon him.
> And I knew him not: but he that sent me to baptize with water, the same said unto me, Upon whom thou shalt see the Spirit descending, and remaining on him, the same is he which baptizeth with the Holy Ghost.
> (John 1:29-33)

Note here that the <u>sin of the world</u> does not refer to the sins of the individuals. In Judaism it is well known that individual sin is addressed at Pesah. This lamb John saw was to be sacrificed for **corporate** sin, the sin of the **world**. The only day on which provision was made for corporate sin was the Day of Atonement - Yom Kippur!

> Know ye not, that so many of us as were baptized into Jesus Christ were baptized into his death?
> Therefore we are buried with him by baptism into death: that like as Christ was raised up from the dead by the glory of the Father, even so we also should walk in newness of life.
> For if we have been planted together in the likeness of his death, we shall be also in the likeness of his resurrection:
> (Romans 6:3-5)

> Buried with him in baptism, wherein also ye are risen with him through the faith of the operation of God, who hath raised him from the dead.
> (Colossians 2:12)

Baptism is called a "burial" in Romans 6:4 and Colossians 2:12. Baptism is "into his death" and involves being "raised to walk in newness of life." In water baptism, immersion portrays burial with Christ, and coming out of the water depicts the resurrection by the power of God to "live a new life". This speaks of being totally immersed in water.

JESUS IN THE WILDERNESS

> Then was Jesus led up of the Spirit into the wilderness to be tempted of the devil.
> And when he had fasted forty days and forty nights, he was afterward an hungred.
> (Matthew 4:1-2)

Jesus was led by the spirit away into a desolate place, inhabited with wild beast in the Judean wilderness. There He ate no food for forty days and nights, an absolute fast and when the fast was completed, Satan come tempting Him. Moses and Elijah both accomplished a forty day fast, it is a remarkable fact that these two men appeared with Christ at His transfiguration.

Those who share Christ's sufferings shall also share His glorification.

> And if children, then heirs; heirs of God, and joint-heirs with Christ; if so be that we suffer with him, that we may be also glorified together.
>
> (Romans 8:17)

> It is a faithful saying: For if we be dead with him, we shall also live with him:
>
> (2 Timothy 2:11)

We know that the first Adam was to abstain from a particular fruit, Christ fasted as to all things edible. The first Adam failed, but Christ the second Adam was victorious

THREE TEMPTATIONS

1. Lust of the flesh

> And when the tempter came to him, he said, If thou be the Son of God, command that these stones be made bread.
>
> (Matthew 4:3)

> But he answered and said, It is written, Man shall not live by bread alone, but by every word that proceedeth out of the mouth of God.
>
> (Matthew 4:4)

Jesus was referring back to Israel's experience in the wilderness

2. Pride of life

Then the devil taketh him up into the holy city, and setteth him on a pinnacle of the temple,

And saith unto him, If thou be the Son of God, cast thyself down: for it is written, He shall give his angels charge concerning thee: and in *their* hands they shall bear thee up, lest at any time thou dash thy foot against a stone.

(Matthew 4:5-6)

Jesus said unto him, It is written again, Thou shalt not tempt the Lord thy God.

(Matthew 4:7)

3. Lust of the eyes

Again, the devil taketh him up into an exceeding high mountain, and sheweth him all the kingdoms of the world, and the glory of them;

And saith unto him, All these things will I give thee, if thou wilt fall down and worship me.

(Matthew 4:8-9)

Then saith Jesus unto him, Get thee hence, Satan: for it is written, Thou shalt worship the Lord thy God, and him only shalt thou serve.

(Matthew 4:10)

Jesus resisted Satan and rebuked him with the Word of God. By using the sword of the Spirit which is the Word of God we too can defeat the devil.

Above all, taking the shield of faith, wherewith ye shall be able to quench all the fiery darts of the wicked.

And take the helmet of salvation, and the sword of the Spirit, which is the word of God:

(Ephesians 4:16-17)

Then the devil leaveth him, and, behold, angels came and ministered unto him.

(Matthew 4:11)

For verily he took not on him the nature of angels; but he took on him the seed of Abraham.

Wherefore in all things it behoved him to be made like unto his brethren, that he might be a merciful and faithful high priest in things pertaining to God, to make reconciliation for the sins of the people.

For in that he himself hath suffered being tempted, he is able to succor them that are tempted.

(Hebrews 2:16-18)

For we have not an high priest which cannot be touched with the feeling of our infirmities; but was in all points tempted like as we are, yet without sin.

(Hebrews 4:15)

JESUS EARLY MINISTRY

In the gospel of John we learn that Jesus returns to where John the Baptist is ministering near Bethany across Jordan at Bethabara. Jesus calls His first disciples, Andrew, who told Simon Peter, his own brother, about Jesus. The following day Jesus called Philip who brought Nathanael (Bartholomew), all from Bethsaida in Galilee. These were common men all called for an uncommon task, to spread the gospel of Christ to the world.

A note about Andrew whom Jesus first called, think about what it would be like today if Jesus had not called Andrew. Would Simon Peter have come to know Jesus? We don't read much about the things that Andrew did personally, but he witnessed to his brother Simon Peter, whose powerful ministry changed the lives of thousands of people. You never know what the outcome will be when you witness to one person, that one person could be, a Simon Peter, the one that turned the world upside down for Jesus.

Jesus' twevle apostles, according to the books of Matthew and Luke in the Bible, were Peter, Andrew, James and John, the son of Zebedee, Philip, Bartholomew, Thomas, Matthew, James the son of Alphaeus, Thaddaeus, Simon and Judas Iscariot. The twelve were among Jesus' closest followers, and spread Christianity after his death, except for Judas Iscariot, whom betray Jesus.

After Judas Iscariot betrays Jesus the disciples chose another to replace him, Matthias was chosen by lot. However some believe the Apostle Paul would have been Jesus selection, and Jesus in fact did call Paul when he was on the road to Damascus, at that time he was known as Saul and had been persecuting the Christians. He was a devoted Pharisee.

All of the disciples came from Galilee except for Judas Iscariot, he was from Kerioth of Judah.

The Talmud says this of the Galileans, "They were more anxious for honor than for gain, quick-tempered, impulsive, emotional, easily aroused by an appeal to adventure, loyal to the end."

I believe this phase describes Peter very well and James and John, the Sons of Thunder, all Jesus disciples were loyal to the end, except for Judas Iscariot, the son of perdition.

Why did Jesus choose Judas? Jesus knew that Judas would betray him yet He chose him as a disciple. Judas was a thief and traitor whom Satan would use to accomplish his work. Jesus had to die for our sins on the cross and Jesus knew what was in Judas's heart. However Satan's plan back fired but Jesus' plan did not. The Bible tells us that Jesus knows our hearts. Jesus knowingly chose Judas and helped arrange His own death for our sake.

THE FIRST MIRACLE OF JESUS

Jesus and His disciples attends a wedding in the town of Cana of Galilee and changes water to wine. A Jewish marriage feast was commonly observed seven to eight days. The Bible tells us there set six water-pots of stone for the purifying of the Jews. They were for the washing of hands before and after eating, tradition of the Pharisees and Jews. (Mark 7:3-4)

His mother saith unto the servants, Whatsoever he saith unto you, do it.

And there were set there six waterpots of stone, after the manner of the purifying of the Jews, containing two or three firkins apiece.

Jesus saith unto them, Fill the waterpots with water. And they filled them up to the brim.

And he saith unto them, Draw out now, and bear unto the governor of the feast. And they bare it.

When the ruler of the feast had tasted the water that was made wine, and knew not whence it was: (but the servants which drew the water knew;) the governor of the feast called the bridegroom,

And saith unto him, Every man at the beginning doth set forth good wine; and when men have well drunk, then that which is worse: but thou hast kept the good wine until now.

This beginning of miracles did Jesus in Cana of Galilee, and manifested forth his glory; and his disciples believed on him.

(John 2:5-11)

Jesus instructed the servants to fill the water pots to the brim with water. Once the pots were filled the servants were instructed by Jesus to draw out a serving and give to the governor of the feast. This is the first of all the miracles Jesus performed and it made believers out of His disciples. I often wondered did the water turn to wine as the servants filled the water pots or when it was drawn out to serve. The Bible doesn't tell us, but it was the best of wines, that it does say.

This miracle, showing Jesus' supernatural control over physical elements like <u>water</u>, marked the beginning of his public ministry. Like his other miracles, it benefited people in need.

Not only did Jesus produce a large quantity of wine, but the quality of it astonished the banquet master. In the same way, Jesus pours his Spirit into us in abundance, giving us God's best.

There is crucial symbolism in this first miracle of Jesus. It was not a coincidence that the water Jesus transformed came from jars used for ceremonial washing. The water signified the Jewish system of purification, and Jesus replaced it with pure wine, representing his spotless blood that would wash away our <u>sins</u>, a much better cleansing.

Jesus travels to Capernaum with family and his disciples from the wedding in Cana, and may have stayed at the home of Peter, whose home was in Capernaum; it was not long until the Feast of Passover. This would be the first Passover Jesus attended after starting His ministry. Jesus drove the money changers and animals out of the temple while in Jerusalem during this Passover. He performed many miracles and the people believed He was a great healer, but not necessarily the Messiah who would save them from sin. Notice in the gospel of John, Jesus is portrayed as the Son of God, His divinity and the Lamb of God. John never uses the name of Mary the mother of Jesus in his gospel. He dwells more on Jesus being the Son of God.

> And the Jews' passover was at hand, and Jesus went up to Jerusalem,
> And found in the temple those that sold oxen and sheep and doves, and the changers of money sitting:
> And when he had made a scourge of small cords, he drove them all out of the temple, and the sheep, and the oxen; and poured out the changers' money, and overthrew the tables;
> And said unto them that sold doves, Take these things hence; make not my Father's house an house of merchandise.
>
> (John 2:13-16)

THE NIGHT VISITOR

Nicodemus was a Pharisee and member of the Sanhedrin; which was a Jewish council of seventy-one members responsible for religious decisions and civil rule. Why did Nicodemus come to see Jesus at night? Was it because of fear of the other council members? Did he want to make sure their conversation would not be interrupted? We don't know, however Nicodemus did not understand what Jesus was talking about when Jesus said "Except a man be born again, he cannot see the kingdom of God." You can read the story in John chapter 3. This is the same Nicodemus that later helped prepare the body of Jesus for burial; we will tell more in a later chapter.

> There was a man of the Pharisees, named Nicodemus, a ruler of the Jews:
>
> The same came to Jesus by night, and said unto him, Rabbi, we know that thou art a teacher come from God: for no man can do these miracles that thou doest, except God be with him.
>
> Jesus answered and said unto him, Verily, verily, I say unto thee, Except a man be born again, he cannot see the kingdom of God.
>
> Nicodemus saith unto him, How can a man be born when he is old? can he enter the second time into his mother's womb, and be born? Jesus answered, Verily, verily, I say unto thee, Except a man be born of water and of the Spirit, he cannot enter into the kingdom of God.
>
> That which is born of the flesh is flesh; and that which is born of the Spirit is spirit.
>
> Marvel not that I said unto thee, Ye must be born again.
>
> (John 3:1-7)

JESUS AND THE SAMARITAN

The Jews would avoid a Samaritan if at all possible; they would have no dealings with them. In traveling from Jerusalem to Galilee, Jews would go around the area where they lived, but Jesus said He <u>must</u> go through Samaria. Didn't He know He would be in territory that Jews normally avoided, that He would perhaps have to deal with them.

Jesus tired and thirsty after coming to Sychar which was in Samaria, sit down by a well. Seeing a Samaritan woman coming to get water Jesus ask her for a drink.

He left Judaea, and departed again into Galilee.

And he <u>must needs</u> go through Samaria.

Then cometh he to a city of Samaria, which is called Sychar, near to the parcel of ground that Jacob gave to his son Joseph.

Now Jacob's well was there. Jesus therefore, being wearied with his journey, sat thus on the well: and it was about the sixth hour.

There cometh a woman of Samaria to draw water: Jesus saith unto her, Give me to drink.

(For his disciples were gone away unto the city to buy meat.)

Then saith the woman of Samaria unto him, How is it that thou, being a Jew, askest drink of me, which am a woman of Samaria? for the Jews have no dealings with the Samaritans.

Jesus answered and said unto her, If thou knewest the gift of God, and who it is that saith to thee, Give me to drink; thou wouldest have asked of him, and he would have given thee living water.

The woman saith unto him, Sir, thou hast nothing to draw with, and the well is deep: from whence then hast thou that living water?

Art thou greater than our father Jacob, which gave us the well, and drank thereof himself, and his children, and his cattle?

Jesus answered and said unto her, Whosoever drinketh of this water shall thirst again:

But whosoever drinketh of the water that I shall give him shall never thirst; but the water that I shall give him shall be in him a well of water springing up into everlasting life.

The woman saith unto him, Sir, give me this water, that I thirst not, neither come hither to draw.

Jesus saith unto her, Go, call thy husband, and come hither.

The woman answered and said, I have no husband. Jesus said unto her, Thou hast well said, I have no husband:

For thou hast had five husbands; and he whom thou now hast is not thy husband: in that saidst thou truly.

The woman saith unto him, Sir, I perceive that thou art a prophet.

Our fathers worshipped in this mountain; and ye say, that in Jerusalem is the place where men ought to worship.

Jesus saith unto her, Woman, believe me, the hour cometh, when ye shall neither in this mountain, nor yet at Jerusalem, worship the Father.

Ye worship ye know not what: we know what we worship: for salvation is of the Jews.

But the hour cometh, and now is, when the true worshippers shall worship the Father in spirit and in truth: for the Father seeketh such to worship him.

God is a Spirit: and they that worship him must worship him in spirit and in truth.

The woman saith unto him, I know that Messias cometh, which is called Christ: when he is come, he will tell us all things.

Jesus saith unto her, I that speak unto thee am he.

(John 4:3-26)

JESUS HOME TOWN REJECTS HIM

Jesus returns to Nazareth, His home town, and went into the synagogue on the Sabbath day and begins to read from Isaiah 61, about the Spirit of the Lord anointing him to preach the good news, heal and set free, and then says, "Today this scripture has been fulfilled in your hearing".

The people of Nazareth could not visualize Jesus other than the young boy that grew up in the home of Joseph, the carpenter. He was just another member of this Nazarene family, the people could not accept Jesus; they were so skeptical Jesus could do no miracles in Nazareth. The people even tried to kill Jesus but He walked away and I can't fine where He ever returns to His home town again.

The Spirit of the Lord is upon me, because he hath anointed me to preach the gospel to the poor; he hath sent me to heal the brokenhearted, to preach deliverance to the captives, and recovering of sight to the blind, to set at liberty them that are bruised, To preach the acceptable year of the Lord...

(Luke 4:18-19)

And he began to say unto them, This day is this scripture fulfilled in your ears.

(Luke 4:21)

And he said unto them, Ye will surely say unto me this proverb, Physician, heal thyself: whatsoever we have heard done in Capernaum, do also here in thy country.

And he said, Verily I say unto you, No prophet is accepted in his own country.

But I tell you of a truth, many widows were in Israel in the days of Elias, when the heaven was shut up three years and six months, when great famine was throughout all the land;

But unto none of them was Elias sent, save unto Sarepta, a city of Sidon, unto a woman that was a widow.

And many lepers were in Israel in the time of Eliseus the prophet; and none of them was cleansed, saving Naaman the Syrian.

(Luke 4:23-27)

And all they in the synagogue, when they heard these things, were filled with wrath,

And rose up, and thrust him out of the city, and led him unto the brow of the hill whereon their city was built, that they might cast him down headlong.

But he passing through the midst of them went his way,

And came down to Capernaum, a city of Galilee, and taught them on the sabbath days.

And they were astonished at his doctrine: for his word was with power.

(Luke 4:28-32)

Jesus's own hometown rejected Him and tried to kill Him, so He left and went to Capernaum and there ministered to the people.

I have mentioned some of the ministry of Jesus when He started at the age of 30, Jesus ministered for three to three and half years, teaching and preaching the Kingdom of heaven was at hand. He healed the sick, the lame, and ministering to every need of the people. John says…

> And there are also many other things which Jesus did, the which, if they should be written every one, I suppose that even the world itself could not contain the books that should be written. Amen.
>
> (John 21:25)

I will not attempt to record all the things written in the Bible about our Lord… I challenge you to read the gospels and learn of the Lord's ministry. Read and let the Holy Spirit speak to you as you study each of the gospels. They paint a perfect picture of Jesus.

- Matthew wrote his gospel to the Jews, from a Jewish viewpoint for a Jewish audience.
- Matthew presented Jesus as the King.
- Mark was written to the Romans, for a gentile audience and portraits Jesus as a Suffering Servant
- Luke, the beloved physician, writing to the Greeks and stressed the humanity of Christ, the Perfect Man which may be why he gave a highly accurate and vividly detailed genealogy of Jesus Christ and account of His birth. Who could better describe the perfect man than a doctor?
- John unveils the man Jesus and reveals Him as the Son of God speaking to non-believers and to the church.

How many times when purchasing a car, a house and etc., do you look only at one side? No you look it over good, the front, the back, each side, inside and out, you want to see all sides of the object. So it is with Jesus, we want to see the entire person, each side and that is what the gospels do.

We see Him as …

- King in Matthews
- Suffering Servant in Mark
- Son of Man in Luke
- Son of God in John

Once again I encourage you to read the gospels, start with John and read Matthews, Mark and Luke. John was wrote to the church and also non-believers, get a good understanding of John and the other gospels will come easy to understand. If John's gospel had a specific purpose statement it would be "that you may believe that Jesus is the Christ, the Son of God, and that by believing you may have life in his name" (John 20:31). The word "believe" appears over 100 times and ties in believe with having eternal life.

The gospels tells us how Jesus healed the sick, made the lame whole, restored the leper, released the demonic, gave life to the dead. He came to give men new life, He was the creator, He was the Son of God, He was the Son of man, and He was the unblemished Lamb of God. He is the Savior of the world, He is our High Priest, He is our King, He is our eternal intercessor interceding for His brethren, He is Alpha and Omega, the beginning and the end, the first and the last.

HE IS ALL IN ALL

To some He is just a fable
To some He is but a mere man
To some He is a babe in a manger
To some He is a carpenter's son
To some He is a great prophet
To some He is a great teacher

He is not a fable
He is not a mere man
He came as a babe in a manger
He was a carpenter's son
He was a great prophet
He was a great teacher

He is truth
He is man sent from God
He is the Bread of Life
He is the Living Water
He is the Messiah
He is the Comforter
He is the Counselor

He is the Prince of Peace
He is the Saviour
He is Lord of All
He is our High Priest
He is the King of kings

He is the Son of God
He is the Everlasting Father
He is the Beginning and the End
He is My Everything
My All in All

By Shirley Ann Baxter Winders

JESUS PRAYS FOR HIS DISCIPLES

And now I am no more in the world, but these are in the world, and I come to thee. Holy Father, keep through thine own name those whom thou hast given me, that they may be one, as we *are*.

While I was with them in the world, I kept them in thy name: those that thou gavest me I have kept, and none of them is lost, but the son of perdition; that the scripture might be fulfilled.

(John 17:11-12)

Chapter 5

THE LAMB OF GOD/ JESUS LAST PASSOVER

It was spring in Jerusalem and the city was alive with thousands of people, Jews from all over the world had gathered for the annual spring feasts of Passover (Pesach) and Unleavened Bread, (a High Sabbath) it was the month of Nisan. This was one of the three pilgrimage feast of the Lords (Leviticus 22-23); the last one our Lord would celebrate with His disciples.

In the Old Testament God gives instructions to Moses for the Passover and Feast of Unleavened Bread.

The key to understanding the timing of Christ's crucifixion and resurrection lies in understanding God's timetable for counting when days begin and end, as well as the timing of His biblical festivals during the spring of the year when these events took place. There were two Sabbaths in that week, with a day of preparation before each of them. John 19:31 tells us that the day Jesus was crucified was a preparation day for a High Day, meaning the next day was a Sabbath celebrating a feast day.

"That Sabbath" was a "high day" and was the "holy convocation"; the first day of the feast, which overshadowed the ordinary weekly Sabbath.

Because there were two Sabbaths in one week has led too much of the confusion about the timing of Jesus's crucifixion. Most people do not recognize the High Sabbath (Unleavened Bread) which fell on Thursday of that week was one of the feast days. They think of the Sabbath as being the weekly Sabbath on Saturday, but that was not the case the week Jesus was crucified, there were two Sabbaths in that week. A High Sabbath and a regular Sabbath on Saturday.

The "high day" of John 19:31 was the first day of the feast on a Thursday, Jesus was crucified on Wednesday the day before the "high day".

> The Jews therefore, because it was the preparation, that the bodies should not remain upon the cross on the sabbath day, (for that sabbath day was an **high day**), besought Pilate that their legs might be broken, and that they might be taken away.
>
> (John 19:31)

The "first day of the feast" was on the 15th day of Nisan and commenced at sunset on what we call the 14th. The Jewish days begin in the evening at sunset and ended the following sunset. "Six days before the passover" (John 12:1) takes us back to the 9th day of Nisan.

> In the fourteenth day of the first month at even is the LORD'S passover.
>
> And on the fifteenth day of the same month is the feast of unleavened bread unto the LORD: seven days ye must eat unleavened bread.
>
> (Leviticus 23:5-6)

> Then Jesus six days before the passover came to Bethany, where Lazarus lived, whom he raised from the dead.
>
> (John 12:1)

> Ye know that after two days is the *feast* of the passover, and the Son of man is betrayed to be crucified.
>
> (Matthew 26:2)

"The first day of the week", the day of the resurrection (Matt. 28:1), was from our Saturday sunset to our Sunday sunset.

> In the end of the sabbath, as it began to dawn toward the first day of the week, came Mary Magdalene and the other Mary to see the sepulchre.
>
> (Matthew 28:1)

Going back from this, "three days and three nights" (Matt. 12:40), we arrive at the day of the burial, which was before sunset, on the 14th of Nisan; before our Wednesday sunset.

> For as Jonas was three days and three nights in the whale's belly; so shall the Son of man be three days and three nights in the heart of the earth.
>
> (Matthew 12:40)

This makes the sixth day before the Passover (the 9th day of Nisan) to be our Thursday sunset to Friday sunset. Therefore Wednesday, Nisan 14th (commencing on our Tuesday at sunset), was "the preparation day", on which the crucifixion took place. All the Gospels agree this was the day the Lord was buried (before our Wednesday sunset), "because it was the preparation day" the bodies should not remain upon the cross on the Sabbath day; "for that Sabbath day was a <u>high day</u>"; therefore, not the ordinary weekly Sabbath.

> The Jews therefore, because it was the preparation, that the bodies should not remain upon the cross on the sabbath day, (for that sabbath day was an high day,) besought Pilate that their legs might be broken, and that they might be taken away.
>
> (John 19:31)

Now Jesus after raising Lazarus from the dead was sought after from that day forward by the chief priests and the Pharisees to kill Him.

> Jesus therefore walked no more openly among the Jews; but went thence unto a country near to the wilderness,

into a city called Ephraim, and there continued with his
disciples.

(John 11:54)

Jesus from the beginning of His ministry spoke of His <u>hour</u> which had not
come, but now was drawing near as Passover was fast approaching and
only then would Jesus offer Himself as the sacrificial lamb of the Passover.
This was God's appointed time for Jesus to give His life as a sacrifice to
save the people. Remember the Feasts of the LORD are appointments God
has set up.

> And the LORD spake unto Moses, saying,
> Speak unto the children of Israel, and say unto them,
> *Concerning* the feasts of the LORD, which ye shall proclaim
> *to be* holy convocations, *even* these *are* my feasts.
>
> (Leviticus 23:1-2)

Every time you see "LORD" or "the LORD" in the Old Testament, it actually
represents the 4-letter name of God (YHWH).

Six days before Passover Jesus returns to the home of Lazarus, whom He
had raised from the dead, and Mary and Martha's and they prepare him
a supper and Mary anoints him with oil, and Jesus sees this as preparing
His body for burial. Reading the gospel of John we learn that Jesus actually
stayed in Bethany during the week of Passover and went back and forth
to Jerusalem.

Four days before Passover Jesus instructs two disciples to go and bring
Him a colt.

> Rejoice greatly, O daughter of Zion; shout, O daughter of
> Jerusalem: behold, thy King cometh unto thee: he is just,
> and having salvation; lowly, and riding upon an ass, and
> upon a colt the foal of an ass.
>
> (Zechariah 9:9)

And when they drew nigh unto Jerusalem, and were come to Bethphage, unto the mount of Olives, then sent Jesus two disciples,

Saying unto them, Go into the village over against you, and straightway ye shall find an ass tied, and a colt with her: loose them, and bring them unto me.

And if any man say ought unto you, ye shall say, The Lord hath need of them; and straightway he will send them.

All this was done, that it might be fulfilled which was spoken by the prophet, saying,

Tell ye the daughter of Sion, Behold, thy King cometh unto thee, meek, and sitting upon an ass, and a colt the foal of an ass.

And the disciples went, and did as Jesus commanded them,

And brought the ass, and the colt, and put on them their clothes, and they set him thereon.

(Matthew 21:1-7)

The symbolism of the donkey may also refer to the Eastern tradition that it is an animal of peace, versus the horse, which is an animal of war. Therefore, a king came riding upon a horse when he was bent on war and rode upon a donkey or mule when he wanted to point out that he was coming in peace. King Solomon, when he was inaugurated as king, rode on a mule, (1Kings 1:33). Therefore, Jesus' entry to Jerusalem symbolized his entry as the *King of Kings, not as a warring king.* It was only proper that the King of Zion should enter into his capital-the city of Jerusalem riding on a donkey. The people praising Him and shouts of Hosanna! Blessed is the one who comes in the name of the Lord THE King of Israel!

The people who expected a great political and military leader would soon be disappointed and turn on Jesus.

FOUR DAYS OF INSPECTION

The sacrificial lamb was lead into the city by the high priest while crowds of worshippers lined the streets waving palm branches and singing Psalm 118, "Blessed is He that comes in the name of the Lord."

It was the day the sacrificial lamb was selected, four days prior to Passover and Jesus is riding into Jerusalem. The same path that the priest brought the sacrificial lamb that was to be inspected and scrutinized for four days as it was tied in the temple prior to being sacrificed. It must be without blemish to be offered to God. Jesus was sending a message to the people and they were expecting to see what they have long hoped for; a Messiah who would restore the kingdom back to Israel. They were hoping to be relieved from the Roman rule that they had been under for the last several years.

They hailed Jesus, King of Kings and the Messiah who would set them free; they did not see Jesus coming as the Suffering Servant who would give His life and free them from their bondage of sin. They quickly turned their backs on Jesus and rejected Him. They wanted freed from the bondage of Roman not from sin.

Jesus was inspected by the Pharisees, the Sadducees, the Herodians and the Scribes who sought to trip him up in His words and entrap Him.

- First challenge...was on the authority of Jesus.
- Second question...concerned paying taxes to Caesar
- Third question... Sadducees concerning the resurrection
- Fourth question... which was the greatest commandment

The conversations with those that tried to entrap Jesus can be found in Mark 12:13-43

They could not trick Jesus with their questions, He was blameless.

Peter and John prepared for the Passover and that evening Jesus and the other disciples gathered to celebrate the Jewish Passover meal. The Jewish Passover meal today is called the "Seder" *(meaning Order)*.

Some people today believe the Last Supper was just another Jewish meal, since it was eaten the day before actual Passover, because Jesus was crucified on Passover at the time the Perpetual Lamb was sacrificed in the Temple at 3:00pm.

If the Last Supper was a regular Jewish meal, and not a Passover meal, "we cannot overlook the significance which Jesus gave to the bread and the wine" during the supper. Jesus used the Passover meal to institute a new memorial meal – a meal to remember Him by. Today the church calls this "communion" which is observed with the breaking of the bread (represents Jesus body) and the wine or grape juice (represents Jesus blood).

> And he said unto them, With desire I have desired to eat this passover with you before I suffer:
>
>> (Luke 22:15)

> And as they were eating, Jesus took bread, and blessed it, and brake it, and gave it to the disciples, and said, Take, eat; this is my body.
>
> And he took the cup, and gave thanks, and gave it to them, saying, Drink ye all of it;
>
> For this is my blood of the new testament, which is shed for many for the remission of sins.
>
> But I say unto you, I will not drink henceforth of this fruit of the vine, until that day when I drink it new with you in my Father's kingdom. (I believe this will be at the marriage supper of the Lamb)
>
> And when they had sung an hymn, they went out into the mount of Olives.
>
>> (Matthew 26:26-30)

> And when he had given thanks, he brake it, and said, Take, eat: this is my body, which is broken for you: this do in remembrance of me.
>
> After the same manner also he took the cup, when he had supped, saying, This cup is the new testament in my blood: this do ye, as oft as ye drink it, in remembrance of me.

> For as often as ye eat this bread, and drink this cup, ye
> do shew the Lord's death till he come.
>
> (1 Corinthians 11:24-26)

Jesus institutes a new covenant – the Jewish Passover (Seder) meal becomes the Lord's Supper (Communion) for the church.

Just as Jews at the Seder discuss the symbolism of the Passover meal, Jesus at his Last Supper discussed the symbolism of the wine and bread in light of his own coming death.

None of the synoptic gospels mention a lamb at the Passover meal Jesus shared with His disciples. Jesus may have wanted it this way, to emphasize the idea that **He** was the Passover sacrifice and by instituting the Lord's Supper. My own thoughts.

> Now when the even was come, he sat down with the twelve.
> And as they did eat, he said, Verily I say unto you, that one of you shall betray me.
> And they were exceeding sorrowful, and began every one of them to say unto him, Lord, is it I?
> And he answered and said, He that dippeth his hand with me in the dish, the same shall betray me.
> The Son of man goeth as it is written of him: but woe unto that man by whom the Son of man is betrayed! it had been good for that man if he had not been born.
> Then Judas, which betrayed him, answered and said, Master, is it I? He said unto him, Thou hast said.
>
> (Matthew 26:20-25)

> Now before the feast of the passover, when Jesus knew that his hour was come that he should depart out of this world unto the Father, having loved his own which were in the world, he loved them unto the end.
> And supper being ended, the devil having now put into the heart of Judas Iscariot, Simon's son, to betray him;
> Jesus knowing that the Father had given all things into his hands, and that he was come from God, and went to God;

> He riseth from supper, and laid aside his garments;
> and took a towel, and girded himself.
> After that he poureth water into a bason, and began to
> wash the disciples' feet, and to wipe them with the towel
> wherewith he was girded.
>
> (John 13:1-5)

"You will note that the word "garments" is plural. In those days men wore three layers of clothing. They wore an outer cape, a sort of long robe that would reach to the ankles; under that they wore a knee-length tunic, and then as an undergarment, they wore a sort of breechcloth. You can gather from this passage that when Jesus began to wash their feet he took off both of his outer garments. He took off his outer robe, the long, flowing robe that he wore, and also the short tunic. So he was dressed in his undergarment -- a breechcloth, the sort of apparel that a servant would wear -- as he washed the disciples' feet.

Paul tells us that Jesus had already laid aside His heavenly garments when He came to earth, now He was laying aside His early garments and only retaining the one garment that a servant would wear for the purpose of washing His disciple's feet.

It was after Jesus had identified Judas and he (Judas) had left the room to carry out his betrayal that Jesus ministered to the eleven disciples to encourage and comfort them concerning the events that were about to take place.

> Ye have heard how I said unto you, I go away, and come
> again unto you. If ye loved me, ye would rejoice, because I
> said, I go unto the Father: for my Father is greater than I.
> And now I have told you before it come to pass, that,
> when it is come to pass, ye might believe.
> Hereafter I will not talk much with you: for the prince
> of this world cometh, and hath nothing in me.
> But that the world may know that I love the Father;
> and as the Father gave me commandment, even so I do.
> Arise, let us go hence.
>
> (John 14:28-31)

Jesus comforts His disciples with the hope of heaven and request love and obedience in John chapter 14 through 16

> I came forth from the Father, and am come into the world: again, I leave the world, and go to the Father.
>
> His disciples said unto him, Lo, now speakest thou plainly, and speakest no proverb.
>
> Now are we sure that thou knowest all things, and needest not that any man should ask thee: by this we believe that thou camest forth from God.
>
> Jesus answered them, Do ye now believe?
>
> Behold, the hour cometh, yea, is now come, that ye shall be scattered, every man to his own, and shall leave me alone: and yet I am not alone, because the Father is with me.
>
> These things I have spoken unto you, that in me ye might have peace. In the world ye shall have tribulation: but be of good cheer; I have overcome the world.
>
> (John 16:28-33)

> Awake, O sword, against my shepherd, and against the man that is my fellow, saith the LORD of hosts: smite the shepherd, and the sheep shall be scattered: and I will turn mine hand upon the little ones.
>
> (Zechariah 13:7)

> Then saith Jesus unto them, All ye shall be offended because of me this night: for it is written, I will smite the shepherd, and the sheep of the flock shall be scattered abroad.
>
> But after I am risen again, I will go before you into Galilee.
>
> (Matthew 26:31-32)

In Matthew 6:9-13 we will find how Jesus tells His disciples how to pray, we call this the Lord's Prayer, but it is really a pattern of how to pray. In John chapter 17 Jesus' prays to the Father. To me this is actually the LORD'S

PRAYER. Jesus is praying to His Father to glorify Him, to preserve His apostles, and all other believers. (See John 17:1-26)

IN THE GARDEN

What a contrast is the garden of Gethsemane where Jesus, the "Second Adam," overcame temptation and submitted to God's will, to the Garden of Eden where Adam and Eve were tempted by Satan and disobeyed God.

Jesus leaving the Upper Room with His disciples withdrew to the Mount of Olives to pray; knowing in a few hours His mission and God's plan of salvation for mankind would be fulfilled. Jesus having His disciples to wait while He continued farther into the garden of Gethsemane to pray and takes with Him Peter, James, and John, who falling asleep gave little support to Jesus. None of the disciples could grasp the reason of His suffering and overcome with fatigue and grief of knowing they were going to lose their closest friend gave in to sleep.

Jesus had urged His disciples to stay awake and pray, if nothing else to pray for their own strength to help them in this time of trial. They failed and fell asleep and later when tested, they fled and scattered as Jesus had told them earlier.

> And they came to a place which was named Gethsemane: and he saith to his disciples, Sit ye here, while I shall pray.
> And he taketh with him Peter and James and John, and began to be sore amazed, and to be very heavy;
> And saith unto them, My soul is exceeding sorrowful unto death: tarry ye here, and watch.
>
> (Mark 14:32-34)

Jesus now was battling the ultimate battle that would deliver all mankind from the power of Satan. His Father would abandon Him while on the cross suffering for our sins. Luke was a physician and he tells us how <u>sweat with drops of blood*</u> fell from his brow while praying in the garden. God's beloved Son whom he loved dearly, yet He gave Him for our sins. Just as an angel was sent to minister to Jesus in the wilderness an angel came to strengthen Him in the garden. Jesus wrestled with His going to the cross, but submitted to the Father's will. (Mark 14:36)

*Hematidrosis** is a rare, but very real, medical condition where one's sweat will contain blood. The sweat glands are surrounded by tiny blood vessels. These vessels can constrict and then dilate to the point of rupture where the blood will then effuse into the sweat glands.

Its cause—*extreme* anguish

> And he said, Abba, Father, all things are possible unto thee; take away this cup from me: nevertheless not what I will, but what thou wilt.
>
> And he cometh, and findeth them sleeping, and saith unto Peter, Simon, sleepest thou? couldest not thou watch one hour?
>
> Watch ye and pray, lest ye enter into temptation. The spirit truly is ready, but the flesh is weak.
>
> And again he went away, and prayed, and spake the same words.
>
> And when he returned, he found them asleep again, (for their eyes were heavy,) neither wist they what to answer him.
>
> And he cometh the third time, and saith unto them, Sleep on now, and take your rest: it is enough, the hour is come; behold, the Son of man is betrayed into the hands of sinners.
>
> Rise up, let us go; lo, he that betrayeth me is at hand.
>
> (Mark 14:36-42)

THE BETRAYAL AND TRIAL

We must understand that the death of Jesus was no accident, but was a vital part of God's divine plan from the very beginning for mankind's redemption. The death of Jesus was orchestrated by the divine Godhead. God's ways are far beyond our ways. God knew what man would do before

He ever created him and planned from the beginning to create a plan to redeem him, which would require a perfect sacrifice.

Judas appeared in the garden with a great multitude and they took Jesus who willingly gave Himself up knowing this was His **time**. Prior scriptures Jesus is noted saying His **time** is not yet, but now His **time** had come for Him to submit to His Father's plan.

> Jesus therefore, knowing all things that should come upon him, went forth, and said unto them, Whom seek ye?
>
> They answered him, Jesus of Nazareth. Jesus saith unto them, I am *he*. And Judas also, which betrayed him, stood with them.
>
> As soon then as *he* had said unto them, I am *he*, they went backward, and fell to the ground.
>
> (John 18:4-6)

You will notice that the word "he" is italicized in the King James Version. If a word is italicized it means that it was not in the original transcript but has been added by the translators thinking it would make the verse clearer. When Jesus answered the soldiers and identifying Himself as I AM (that is God's name) remember in Exodus when Moses ask God at the burning bush, "Who shall I say sent me?" God said tell them I AM that I AM. Could it be the power of God's name that forced the soldiers backward could it mean He was in control and the arrest was allowed to fulfill God's plan of salvation? Yes, I believe so.

> And God said unto Moses, I AM THAT I AM: and he said, Thus shalt thou say unto the children of Israel, I AM hath sent me unto you.
>
> (Exodus 3:14)

The disciples fled and Jesus was led by the soldiers to Annas and then to Caiaphas, the high priest.

Jesus stands trial before the Sanhedrin, a Jewish judicial body, following his arrest in the garden. Now there was one disciple, Peter who follow Jesus afar off. Jesus had told Peter he would deny him three times before the cockcrow twice. Mark 14:66-72 tells of the denials of Peter.

> Jesus said unto him, Verily I say unto thee, That this night, before the cock crow, thou shalt deny me thrice.
>
> (Matthew 26:34)

THE NIGHT WATCH IN THE CENTURY

1. Sundown to 9 pm   first watch
2. 9 pm to midnight   second watch
3. Midnight to 3 am   third watch (the cockcrow, "*gallicinium*")
4. 3 am to sun rise   fourth watch

The end of each watch was signaled by the sound of a trumpet as Jesus noted in Mark 13:35:

So stay awake, because you do not know when the master of the house is coming: evening, midnight, cockcrow or dawn.

A trumpet was blown to signal the end of each Watch and the change of the guard. The Romans called the trumpet blast at the end of the Third Watch the *"gallicinium,"* in Latin, "cockcrow." Jesus was referring to the *gallicinium* in Latin or *alektorophonia* in Greek, when He told Peter he would deny Him before the cockcrow. His time reference was to the trumpet signal of the "cockcrow" that was a precise military signal, and Peter denied Christ exactly as Jesus had said.

> Watch ye therefore: for ye know not when the master of the house cometh, at even, or at midnight, or at the cockcrowing, or in the morning:
>
> (Mark 13:35)

There were six parts to Jesus' trial: three stages in a religious court and three stages before a Roman court. Jesus was tried before Annas, the former high priest; Caiaphas, the current high priest; and the Sanhedrin. He was charged in these trials with blasphemy, claiming to be the Son of God.

Jesus did not defend, and rarely responded to the accusations; He was condemned by the Jewish authorities when he did not deny that he was the Son of God. The Jewish leaders then take Jesus to Pontius Pilate, the governor appointed by Roman to Judaea, and ask that he be tried for claiming to be the King of the Jews.

> And the men that held Jesus mocked him, and smote him.
>
> And when they had blindfolded him, they struck him on the face, and asked him, saying, Prophesy, who is it that smote thee?
>
> And many other things blasphemously spake they against him.
>
> And as soon as it was day, the elders of the people and the chief priests and the scribes came together, and led him into their council, saying,
>
> Art thou the Christ? tell us. And he said unto them, If I tell you, ye will not believe:
>
> And if I also ask you, ye will not answer me, nor let me go.
>
> Hereafter shall the Son of man sit on the right hand of the power of God.
>
> Then said they all, Art thou then the Son of God? And he said unto them, Ye say that I am.
>
> And they said, What need we any further witness? for we ourselves have heard of his own mouth.
>
> (Luke 22:63-71)

> And Pilate asked him, saying, Art thou the King of the Jews? And he answered him and said, Thou sayest it.
>
> Then said Pilate to the chief priests and to the people, I find no fault in this man.
>
> (Luke 23:3-4)

Just as the high priest would confirm the sacrificial lamb being examined for four days, he would say I find no found in him, Pilot also stated that he found no fault in Jesus.

Pontius Pilate who found no fault in Jesus and would have let Him go free if it had not been for the Jews insisting Jesus be killed. But when Pontius Pilate heard Jesus was from Galilee, he send Him to King Herod (Herod was tetrarch of Galilee) this was the son of Herod the Great who have tried to kill Jesus as a child.

> And they were the more fierce, saying, He stirreth up the people, teaching throughout all Jewry, beginning from Galilee to this place.
>
> When Pilate heard of Galilee, he asked whether the man were a Galilaean.
>
> And as soon as he knew that he belonged unto Herod's jurisdiction, he sent him to Herod, who himself also was at Jerusalem at that time.
>
> And when Herod saw Jesus, he was exceeding glad: for he was desirous to see him of a long season, because he had heard many things of him; and he hoped to have seen some miracle done by him.
>
> Then he questioned with him in many words; but he answered him nothing.
>
> And the chief priests and scribes stood and vehemently accused him.
>
> And Herod with his men of war set him at nought, and mocked him, and arrayed him in a gorgeous robe, and sent him again to Pilate.
>
> And the same day Pilate and Herod were made friends together: for before they were at enmity between themselves.
>
> (Luke 23:5-12)

There were many illegalities that took place in these trials from the perspective of Jewish law:

- No trial was to be held during feast time.
- Each member of the court was to vote individually to convict or acquit, but Jesus was convicted by acclamation.

- If the death penalty was given, a night must pass before the sentence was carried out; however, only a few hours passed before Jesus was placed on the Cross.
- The Jews had no authority to execute anyone.
- No trial was to be held at night, but this trial was held before dawn.
- The accused was to be given counsel or representation, but Jesus had none.
- The accused was not to be asked self-incriminating questions, but Jesus was asked if He was the Christ.

Second time before Pilate, Jesus being sent back to him from King Herod after the soldiers had mocked Jesus and placing a royal robe on Him calling Him King of the Jews. They ridiculed and spit upon Jesus, He was beaten with a cat of nine tails. Scourging was a brutal punishment, but it was standard practice before a crucifixion. The whip, the *flagellum*, had several thongs, each one of which had pieces of bone or metal attached. It made a bloody pulp of a man's body.

The person to be whipped was stripped of his clothing, tied to a post or pillar, and beaten until his flesh hung in shreds.

The trials before the Roman authorities started with Pilate after Jesus was beaten. Pilate found no reason to kill Jesus so he sent Him to Herod (Luke 23:7). Herod had Jesus ridiculed but, wanting to avoid the political liability, sent Jesus back to Pilate (Luke 23:11–12). This was the last trial as Pilate tried to appease the animosity of the Jews by having Jesus scourged. The Roman scourge was a terrible whipping designed to remove the flesh from the back of the one being punished. In a final effort to have Jesus released, Pilate offered the prisoner Barabbas to be crucified and Jesus released, but to no avail. The crowds called for Barabbas to be released and Jesus to be crucified. Pilate granted their demand and surrendered Jesus to their will. The trials of Jesus represent the ultimate mockery of justice, who was found guilty of crimes he never committed and sentenced to death by crucifixion.

***We owed a debt we could not pay, He paid a debt He did not owe.
This is unconditional love***

God gave His only son that we may have life and have it abundantly. Jesus paid a debt He did not owe to save mankind from eternal damnation. No greater love hath any man than the love of Jesus.

> These words spake Jesus, and lifted up his eyes to heaven, and said, Father, the hour is come; glorify thy Son, that thy Son also may glorify thee:
>
> As thou hast given him power over all flesh, that he should give eternal life to as many as thou hast given him.
>
> And this is life eternal, that they might know thee the only true God, and Jesus Christ, whom thou hast sent.
>
> I have glorified thee on the earth: I have finished the work which thou gavest me to do.
>
> And now, O Father, glorify thou me with thine own self with the glory which I had with thee before the world was.
>
> (John 17:1-5)

THE DAY JESUS DIED/THE ULTIMATE SACRIFICE

> And they bring him unto the place Golgotha, which is, being interpreted, The place of a skull.
>
> And they gave him to drink wine mingled with myrrh: but he received it not.
>
> And when they had crucified him, they parted his garments, casting lots upon them, what every man should take.
>
> And it was the **third hour,** and they crucified him.
>
> And the superscription of his accusation was written over, THE KING OF THE JEWS.
>
> And with him they crucify two thieves; the one on his right hand, and the other on his left.
>
> And the scripture was fulfilled, which saith, And he was numbered with the transgressors.
>
> And they that passed by railed on him, wagging their heads, and saying, Ah, thou that destroyest the temple, and buildest it in three days,
>
> Save thyself, and come down from the cross.

Likewise also the chief priests mocking said among themselves with the scribes, He saved others; himself he cannot save.

Let Christ the King of Israel descend now from the cross, that we may see and believe. And they that were crucified with him reviled him.

And when the **sixth hour** was come, there was darkness over the whole land until the **ninth hour.**

And at the **ninth hour** Jesus cried with a loud voice, saying, Eloi, Eloi, lama sabachthani? which is, being interpreted, My God, my God, why hast thou forsaken me?

And some of them that stood by, when they heard it, said, Behold, he calleth Elias.

And one ran and filled a spunge full of vinegar, and put it on a reed, and gave him to drink, saying, Let alone; let us see whether Elias will come to take him down.

And Jesus cried with a loud voice, and gave up the ghost.

And the veil of the temple was rent in twain from the top to the bottom.

(Mark 15:22-38)

The Jewish daytime hours began with dawn and ended with sundown, which began the next day. The hours are seasonal, so the length of the daylight hours varied with the season of the year. The Romans began their day at midnight, as we do and counted twelve hours to twelve noon and then twelve more hours from noon to the midnight.

THIRD HOUR 9-10 am - the first lamb was sacrificed in the Temple
SIXTH HOUR 12-1 pm - darkness covered the whole land until the ninth hour
NINTH HOUR 3-4 pm - Jesus died and the veil in the temple was rent top to bottom

<u>Why the darkness?</u> In the Old Testament often darkness was associated with God's judgment. This was a physical manifestation of God's judgment of His Son. Jesus was being forsaken and condemned by His Father, not because He was a sinner, but because He was bearing our sins. God cannot

look on sin and because Jesus took our sins and died for us that we might be saved, God the Father could not look upon His Son.

> And when the sixth hour was come, there was darkness over the whole land until the ninth hour.
> And at the ninth hour Jesus cried with a loud voice, saying, Eloi, Eloi, lama sabachthani? which is, being interpreted, My God, my God, why hast thou forsaken me?
> (Mark 15:33-34)

Why was the veil rent? Jesus cried with a shout of victory…."it is finished!" or Paid in full (tetelestai). Jesus paid the sin debt by giving His life as a perfect sacrificial substitute. The veil separated the people from the presence of God because of sin. Only once a year could the high priest enter into the Holy of Holies with the blood of the blameless animal substitute to offer it in symbolic payment for the people's sins. The death of Jesus now fulfilled that symbolic sacrifice, we are now no longer under the law, but under God's grace. Jesus is now our high priest standing by the right side of God and ever interceding for us daily. We don't have to wait a year to talk to God, we can enter into His presence anytime.

> And Jesus cried with a loud voice, and gave up the ghost.
> And the veil of the temple was rent in twain from the top to the bottom.
> And when the centurion, which stood over against him, saw that he so cried out, and gave up the ghost, he said, Truly this man was the Son of God.
> (Mark 15:37-39)

Why the earthquake? The Bible states that the graves were opened at the time of the earthquake (at Jesus death), but the people did not come forth until after Jesus was resurrected. The Bible does not tell us who these people were, but that they were saints, whether they were Old Testament saints or believers who died before Jesus's crucifixion, we do not know. Were they raised to life like Lazarus to die again, or raised to be taken to heaven with Jesus. The Bible does not tell us these things, was this a fulfillment of the Old Testament feast of the first-fruits (Lev. 23:10-14)? Was this resurrection of the saints' evidence of the coming harvest when Jesus returns to rapture His church?

> But now is Christ risen from the dead, and become the firstfruits of them that slept.
>
> For since by man came death, by man came also the resurrection of the dead.
>
> For as in Adam all die, even so in Christ shall all be made alive.
>
> But every man in his own order: Christ the firstfruits; afterward they that are Christ's at his coming.
>
> (1 Corinthians 15:20-23)

There are different views as to the day Jesus actually died, some believe it Friday, some Thursday and some Wednesday. Let's take a look at what the Gospel of John tells us. John 19:31 tells us that Jesus was crucified on a preparation day of a High Sabbath, we must understand that the Jews celebrated a weekly Sabbath and also the Feasts of the Lords, which could fall on a weekday other than the regular weekly Sabbath. You could have two Sabbaths, in one week, a High Sabbath (a feast day) and the regular weekly Sabbath. This is what happen the week Jesus was crucified, as was mentioned earlier. Now Joseph of Arimathea ask Pilate for the body of Jesus on the preparation of the High Sabbath that he might prepare Jesus' body and laid Him in the tomb before the High Sabbath began, which happened to be on Thursday of that week.

> The Jews therefore, because it was the preparation, that the bodies should not remain upon the cross on the sabbath day, (for that sabbath day was an high day,) besought Pilate that their legs might be broken, and that they might be taken away.
>
> (John 19:31)

> And he made his grave with the wicked, and with the rich in his death; because he had done no violence, neither was any deceit in his mouth.
>
> (Isaiah 53:9)

And after this Joseph of Arimathaea, being a disciple of Jesus, but secretly for fear of the Jews, besought Pilate that he might take away the body of Jesus: and Pilate gave him leave. He came therefore, and took the body of Jesus.

And there came also Nicodemus, which at the first came to Jesus by night, and brought a mixture of myrrh and aloes, about an hundred pound weight.

Then took they the body of Jesus, and wound it in linen clothes with the spices, as the manner of the Jews is to bury.

Now in the place where he was crucified there was a garden; and in the garden a new sepulchre, wherein was never man yet laid.

There laid they Jesus therefore because of the Jews' preparation day; for the sepulchre was nigh at hand.

(John 19:38-42)

And now when the even was come, because it was the preparation, that is, the day before the Sabbath,

Joseph of Arimathaea, an honourable counsellor, which also waited for the kingdom of God, came, and went in boldly unto Pilate, and craved the body of Jesus.

And Pilate marvelled if he were already dead: and calling unto him the centurion, he asked him whether he had been any while dead.

And when he knew it of the centurion, he gave the body to Joseph.

And he bought fine linen, and took him down, and wrapped him in the linen, and laid him in a sepulchre which was hewn out of a rock, and rolled a stone unto the door of the sepulchre.

And Mary Magdalene and Mary the mother of Joses beheld where he was laid.

(Mark 15:42-47)

And, behold, there was a man named Joseph, a counsellor; and he was a good man, and a just:

(The same had not consented to the counsel and deed of them;) he was of Arimathaea, a city of the Jews: who also himself waited for the kingdom of God.

This man went unto Pilate, and begged the body of Jesus.

And he took it down, and wrapped it in linen, and laid it in a sepulchre that was hewn in stone, wherein never man before was laid.

And that day was the preparation, and the sabbath drew on.

And the women also, which came with him from Galilee, followed after, and beheld the sepulchre, and how his body was laid.

And they returned, and prepared spices and ointments; and rested the sabbath day according to the commandment.

(Luke 23:50-56)

Mark and Luke also confirms it was the day before the Sabbath, they do not specify a High Sabbath, but John does, we must search all the scriptures to get a full understanding of what is taking place.

Luke tells us that the women followed to the tomb and after Jesus was laid, they (the women) returned and prepared spices and ointments to go back to the tomb. Why did they not go back to the tomb that night? Because the High Sabbath (Passover) had started. Jesus had been arrested very early in the morning on Wednesday (Preparation day) had gone through all the trials and was on the cross by 9:00 am Wednesday morning.

And when the sabbath was past (this was the weekly Sabbath), Mary Magdalene, and Mary the mother of James, and Salome, had bought sweet spices, that they might come and anoint him.

And very early in the morning the first day of the week, (Sunday) they came unto the sepulchre at the rising of the sun.

And they said among themselves, Who shall roll us away the stone from the door of the sepulchre?

(Mark 16:1-3)

Mark 16:1-3 says when the Sabbath was past, the women came very early in the morning the first day of the week (this would be Sunday).

So we have a day of...

- Preparation of the High Sabbath - Day Jesus was crucified and body laid in tomb.
- The High Sabbath - they rested
- The day between the High Sabbath and the Sabbath in Marks gospel - Friday
- Why did the women not go to the tomb on Friday? The tomb was guarded by Roman soldiers they would have been arrested.
- Why did they wait till Sunday? Because Saturday was the weekly Sabbath.

We find that...

- Wednesday - was preparation day of the High Sabbath
- Thursday was High Sabbath (Passover/Feast of Unleavened Bread) – no work
- Friday - soldiers guarded the tomb
- Saturday weekly Sabbath – no work
- Sunday 1st day of the week - Jesus had risen

> For as Jonas was three days and three nights in the whale's belly; so shall the Son of man be three days and three nights in the heart of the earth.
>
> (Matthew 12:40)

Jesus was in the earth three days and three nights just as He said He would be and rose just before Sunday the first day of the week... Jewish days begin around 6:00 pm

1.	Wednesday - Thursday	night	day	6 pm – 6 pm
2.	Thursday - Friday	night	day	6 pm – 6 pm
3.	Friday - Saturday	night	day	6 pm – 6 pm

And God called the light Day, and the darkness he called Night. And the evening and the morning were the first day.

(Genesis 1:5)

Jewish day was sunset to sunset. Our days are midnight to midnight. Did you ever wonder how you could fit three days and three nights between Friday night and Sunday morning?

I believe the Gospels support that Jesus was crucified on Wednesday, the day before the High Sabbath. That He rose just as the first day was dawning, when Mary got to the tomb Jesus was already risen. The stone had been rolled away not to let Jesus out, but to let others see He was not there. JESUS AROSE, HE IS ALIVE FOR EVERMORE.

Now when Jesus <u>was risen early the first day of the week</u>, he appeared first to Mary Magdalene, out of whom he had cast seven devils.

(Mark 16:9)

CHRIST AROSE

In the end of the sabbath, as it began to <u>dawn toward the first day of the week</u>, came Mary Magdalene and the other Mary to see the sepulchre.

And, behold, there was a great earthquake: for the angel of the Lord descended from heaven, and came and rolled back the stone from the door, and sat upon it.

His countenance was like lightning, and his raiment white as snow:

And for fear of him the keepers did shake, and became as dead men.

And the angel answered and said unto the women, Fear not ye: for I know that ye seek Jesus, which was crucified.

He is not here: for he is risen, as he said. Come, see the place where the Lord lay.

(Matthew 28:1-6)

And when the sabbath was past, Mary Magdalene, and Mary the mother of James, and Salome, had bought sweet spices, that they might come and anoint him.

And very early in the morning the first day of the week, they came unto the sepulchre at the rising of the sun.

And they said among themselves, Who shall roll us away the stone from the door of the sepulchre?

And when they looked, they saw that the stone was rolled away: for it was very great.

And entering into the sepulchre, they saw a young man sitting on the right side, clothed in a long white garment; and they were affrighted.

And he saith unto them, Be not affrighted: Ye seek Jesus of Nazareth, which was crucified: he is risen; he is not here: behold the place where they laid him.

(Mark 16:1-6)

Now upon the first day of the week, very early in the morning, they came unto the sepulchre, bringing the spices which they had prepared, and certain others with them.

And they found the stone rolled away from the sepulchre.

And they entered in, and found not the body of the Lord Jesus.

And it came to pass, as they were much perplexed thereabout, behold, two men stood by them in shining garments:

And as they were afraid, and bowed down their faces to the earth, they said unto them, Why seek ye the living among the dead?

He is not here, but is risen: remember how he spake unto you when he was yet in Galilee,

Saying, The Son of man must be delivered into the hands of sinful men, and be crucified, and the third day rise again.

And they remembered his words,

And returned from the sepulchre, and told all these things unto the eleven, and to all the rest.

It was Mary Magdalene, and Joanna, and Mary the mother of James, and other women that were with them, which told these things unto the apostles.

(Luke 24:1-10)

But Mary stood without at the sepulchre weeping: and as she wept, she stooped down, and looked into the sepulchre,

And seeth two angels in white sitting, the one at the head, and the other at the feet, where the body of Jesus had lain.

And they say unto her, Woman, why weepest thou? She saith unto them, Because they have taken away my Lord, and I know not where they have laid him.

And when she had thus said, she turned herself back, and saw Jesus standing, and knew not that it was Jesus.

Jesus saith unto her, Woman, why weepest thou? whom seekest thou? She, supposing him to be the gardener, saith unto him, Sir, if thou have borne him hence, tell me where thou hast laid him, and I will take him away.

Jesus saith unto her, Mary. She turned herself, and saith unto him, Rabboni; which is to say, Master.

Jesus saith unto her, Touch me not; for I am not yet ascended to my Father: but go to my brethren, and say unto them, I ascend unto my Father, and your Father; and to my God, and your God.

Mary Magdalene came and told the disciples that she had seen the Lord, and that he had spoken these things unto her.

(John 20:11-18)

Why the two angels sitting one at each end of the place where Jesus had laid in the tomb?

- Angels predicted the birth of Jesus to Mary and Joseph
- Angels announced His birth to the shepherds.
- Angels were involved in various aspects of Jesus life.
- Angels ministered to Jesus in the wilderness and in Gethsemane.

These <u>two</u> angels were the first to officially announce that Jesus had arose and angels will accompany Jesus when He returns.

> It is also written in your law, that the testimony of <u>two</u> men is true.
>
> (John 8:17)

THE BLOOD OF JESUS

Mary Magdalene was the first to see Jesus after He had risen from the grave, but He had not yet ascended to His Father. "Touch me not" Jesus said unto her, why did Jesus say this to Mary?

We must look back into the Old Testament, when the high priest would go into the holy of holies once a year to atone for the sins of Israel.

In the Old Testament, the high priest would go into the Holy of Holies once a year to atone for the sins of the people. He purified himself and he could not be touched by anyone prior to entering the Holy of Holies to make atonement for the people. He would sprinkle the blood seven times on the mercy seat to atone for the sins of the Israel.

As our high priest, Christ entered heaven after His resurrection and offered his own blood to procure pardon for us. Having offered a "better sacrifice", he did not need to offer himself but one time. He put away sin, won the victory, by the sacrifice of himself, this was prefigured by the Tabernacle and Temple in the Old Testament. It is impossible for the blood of animals to take away sin (Heb. 10:4).

The blood of the sacrifice was sprinkled before the veil seven times, signifying this—first, that the atonement made by the blood of Jesus is perfect in its reference to God.

Not only is the atonement perfect, but the presentation is perfect. Christ presented Himself as a perfect sacrifice for sin. As it was written concerning the Passover, "When I see the blood, I will pass over you." Jesus completely paid the price for our sins in full, all we have to do is accept Him and obey Him.

Jesus could not have been touched by any human, including Mary, before He ascended and presented His blood in the tabernacle in heaven, or He could not have been accepted as our sacrifice for sin.

> For Christ is not entered into the holy places made with hands, which are the figures of the true; but into heaven itself, now to appear in the presence of God for us:
> Nor yet that he should offer himself often, as the high priest entereth into the holy place every year with blood of others...
>
> (Hebrews 9:24-25)

Jesus made one offering for our sins, no longer were there to be sacrifices repeated time after time. Jesus was the ultimate sacrifice for all eternity.

> Now of the things which we have spoken this is the sum: We have such an high priest, who is set on the right hand of the throne of the Majesty in the heavens;
> A minister of the sanctuary, and of the true tabernacle, which the Lord pitched, and not man.
> For every high priest is ordained to offer gifts and sacrifices: wherefore it is of necessity that this man have somewhat also to offer.
> For if he were on earth, he should not be a priest, seeing that there are priests that offer gifts according to the law:
> Who serve unto the example and shadow of heavenly things, as Moses was admonished of God when he was about to make the tabernacle: for, See, saith he, that thou make all things according to the pattern shewed to thee in the mount.
>
> (Hebrews 8:1-5.)

Remember God told Moses to build the tabernacle exactly as He showed him in the pattern when Moses was on top of Mt. Sinai. There is a true tabernacle in heaven and that is where Jesus was going to place His blood upon the true mercy seat before His Father in heaven when Mary met Him in the garden.

If Mary had touched Jesus, the blood sacrifice would have been tainted with corruption. Jesus was heading towards heaven with the blood which needed to be applied to the mercy seat in Heaven to cover our sins.

> Seeing then that we have a great high priest, that is passed into the heavens, Jesus the Son of God, let us hold fast our profession.
>
> For we have not an high priest which cannot be touched with the feeling of our infirmities; but was in all points tempted like as we are, yet without sin.
>
> Let us therefore come boldly unto the throne of grace, that we may obtain mercy, and find grace to help in time of need.
>
> (Hebrews 4:14-16)

The veil has been rent and we can come boldly before the throne of God with our praise and partitions. Jesus fulfilled everything that God had required for salvation. He was perfect and sinless as He lived here on earth, He kept the law, shed His blood and rose again to go to the heavenly temple and offer the blood (His blood) as an atonement for our sins once and for all. A new covenant, we are no longer under the law, but under Grace.

- Grace is getting what we do not deserve.
- Mercy is not getting what we deserve.

The Ark was an important foreshadowing of Jesus Christ as the sole place of atonement for sins. As the Ark was the only place Old Testament believers could go (through the high priest) to have their sins forgiven, so Christ is now the only way to salvation and the kingdom of heaven.

This ministry of the blood by the priest foreshadowed Jesus' presenting His blood for us in heaven. After Jesus died on the cross as our sacrifice for sin, He arose and went to heaven as our priest to minister His blood in the heavenly sanctuary. The blood ministered by the earthly priest represents

Jesus applying His blood to our record of sins in the sanctuary above, showing that they are forgiven when we confess them in His name.

> But Christ being come an high priest of good things to come, by a greater and more perfect tabernacle, not made with hands, that is to say, not of this building;
> Neither by the blood of goats and calves, but by his own blood he entered in once into the holy place, having obtained eternal redemption *for us*.
>
> (Hebrews 9:11-12)

> If we confess our sins, he is faithful and just to forgive us *our* sins, and to cleanse us from all unrighteousness.
>
> (1 John 1:9)

The Old Testament offering for the sins of Israel

> And he shall take of the blood of the bullock, and sprinkle *it* with his finger upon the mercy seat eastward; and before the mercy seat shall he sprinkle of the blood with his finger **seven times**.
>
> (Leviticus 16:14)

Jesus shed His blood seven places on His body...

1. Head (crown of thorns)
2. Right hand – (nails)
3. Left hand – (nails)
4. Back (stripes)
5. Side (sword pierced)
6. Right food (nails)
7. Left foot (nails)

The number 7 in the Bible stands for completion. Jesus paid our sins in full when He said "It is Finished."

But Christ being come an high priest of good things to come, by a greater and more perfect tabernacle, not made with hands, that is to say, not of this building;

Neither by the blood of goats and calves, but by his own blood he entered in once into the holy place, having obtained eternal redemption for us.

(Hebrews 9:11-12)

For anyone to teach that Jesus' blood has no redeeming power is a false prophet. To make light the necessity of Christ's blood sacrifice is an abomination unto God. After Jesus appeared before His Father in heaven, He manifested Himself over a forty day period, to teach and train His apostles, twelve common men to evangelize the world.

Until the day in which he was taken up, after that he through the Holy Ghost had given commandments unto the apostles whom he had chosen:

To whom also he shewed himself alive after his passion by many infallible proofs, being seen of them forty days, and speaking of the things pertaining to the kingdom of God:

And, being assembled together with them, commanded them that they should not depart from Jerusalem, but wait for the promise of the Father, which, saith he, ye have heard of me.

For John truly baptized with water; but ye shall be baptized with the Holy Ghost not many days hence.

(Acts 1:2-5)

And it came to pass in those days, that he went out into a mountain to pray, and continued all night in prayer to God.

And when it was day, he called unto him his disciples: and of them he chose twelve, whom also he named apostles;

Simon, (whom he also named Peter,) and Andrew his brother, James and John, Philip and Bartholomew,

Matthew and Thomas, James the son of Alphaeus, and Simon called Zelotes,

> And Judas the brother of James, and Judas Iscariot,
> which also was the traitor.
>
> (Luke 6:12-16)

A disciple is a student, someone who learns, not only that but in Jesus time, a disciple followed their teacher. These twelve men had been with Jesus before His death and resurrection, but now there must be intense teaching and training, and only forty days to do it in, before Jesus would leave them to return to heaven. Of the first four, Andrew, Peter, and James and John we know they were two sets of brothers who were fishermen. The other eight we know little about them except for their names. Matthew was a Roman tax collector, who was despised by the Jews. Simon the Cananite, was a Zealot who hated the Romans. Little is known of their personal lives, Cananite had nothing to do with geography but was a Hebrew word for "zealous," identifying Simon as a member of the radical Zealot party. What a contrast of men, the disciples were, none of them associated with the religious group of the Jews who ruled in the religious realm in Jesus day. Not a Pharisee or Sadducee was chosen. They were all from Galilee except for Judas Iscariot, who was from Kerioth in Judean.

Josephus says the Zealots were reckless persons, zealous in good practices and extravagant and reckless in the worst kind of actions.

Why did Jesus chose Judas Iscariot?

A man once asked a theologian, "Why did Jesus choose Judas Iscariot to be his disciple?" The teacher replied, "I don't know, but I have an even harder question: Why did Jesus choose me?"

Did Jesus choose a traitor knowingly? Yes, He knew that Judas was precisely the sort of man who would push Him toward the cross. In selecting him He helped arrange His own death – for our sake. It was in God's plan from the beginning of time. God is Omnipotent (all powerful), Omnipresent (everywhere) and omniscient (all knowing).

> Yea, mine own familiar friend, in whom I trusted, which
> did eat of my bread, hath lifted up his heel against me.
>
> (Psalm 41:9)

I speak not of you all: I know whom I have chosen: <u>but that the scripture may be fulfilled, He that eateth bread with me hath lifted up his heel against me.</u>

Now I tell you before it come, that, when it is come to pass, ye may believe that I am he.

Verily, verily, I say unto you, He that receiveth whomsoever I send receiveth me; and he that receiveth me receiveth him that sent me.

When Jesus had thus said, he was troubled in spirit, and testified, and said, Verily, verily, I say unto you, that one of you shall betray me.

Then the disciples looked one on another, doubting of whom he spake.

(John 13:18-22)

Jesus answered them, Have not I chosen you twelve, and one of you is a devil?

He spake of Judas Iscariot the son of Simon: for he it was that should betray him, being one of the twelve.

(John 6:70-71)

While I was with them in the world, I kept them in thy name: those that thou gavest me I have kept, and none of them is lost, but the son of perdition; that the scripture might be fulfilled.

(John 17:12)

Just because someone says they are a Christian or goes to church does not make them a Christian. 1 John 2:19 explains why some do not remain. I have often said that going to church doesn't make me a Christian any more than going to the garage makes me a car.

They went out from us, but they were not of us; for if they had been of us, they would no doubt have continued with us: but they went out, that they might be made manifest that they were not all of us.

(1 John 2:19)

The last words of Jesus talking with His apostles...

> And he said unto <u>them</u> (the apostles), It is not for you to know the times or the seasons, which the Father hath put in his own power.
> But <u>ye</u> (the apostles) shall receive power, after that the Holy Ghost is come upon <u>you </u> (the apostles): and <u>ye</u> (the apostles) shall be witnesses unto me both in Jerusalem, and in all Judaea, and in Samaria, and unto the uttermost part of the earth.
>
> (Acts 1:7-8; my emphasis)

Remember these verses when we get to Acts chapter 2

Chapter 6

JESUS ASCENSION TO HEAVEN/PROMISE OF THE FATHER

This was forty days after His resurrection as Jesus ascended to heaven, leaving His apostles to wait for the Father's Promise.

> And when he had spoken these things, while they beheld, he was taken up; and a cloud received him out of their sight.
>
> And while they looked stedfastly toward heaven as he went up, behold, two men stood by them in white apparel;
>
> Which also said, Ye men of Galilee, why stand ye gazing up into heaven? This same Jesus, which is taken up from you into heaven, shall so come in like manner as ye have seen him go into heaven.
>
> (Acts 1:9-11)

Jesus had finished His earthly work and just before He died on the cross He said "It is finished". The debt was paid. The ascension signifies that the Father accepted the work of his Son, Jesus who is now our high priest in heaven.

If you are in Christ you have His promise that your body will be renewed and gloriously raised in the resurrection. Then we all shall see him as he is, and we will be with him forever. The ascension guarantees our Christian destiny, because he was raised, we too will be raised, because he ascended, we too will ascend, because he is in heaven, we will join him there someday.

Let not your heart be troubled: ye believe in God, believe also in me.

In my Father's house are many mansions: if it were not so, I would have told you. I go to prepare a place for you.

And if I go and prepare a place for you, I will come again, and receive you unto myself; that where I am, there ye may be also.

(John 14:1-3)

THE APOSTLES WAIT IN JERUSALEM

Jesus gave His apostles instructions to not leave Jerusalem, but wait there until they received the Promise of the Father. The very place where Jesus was crucified, where his greatest enemies were, where Jesus had suffered the most reproach. It was here in Jerusalem that Peter, the one in this very city had denied Jesus, now he would preach his first sermon empowered by the Holy Spirit. 3000 souls would be saved and the beginning of the church.

And that repentance and remission of sins should be preached in his name among all nations, beginning at Jerusalem.

And ye are witnesses of these things.

And, behold, I send the promise of my Father upon you: but tarry ye in the city of Jerusalem, until ye be endued with power from on high.

And he led them out as far as to Bethany, and he lifted up his hands, and blessed them.

And it came to pass, while he blessed them, he was parted from them, and carried up into heaven.

And they worshipped him, and returned to Jerusalem with great joy:

> And were continually in the temple, praising and
> blessing God. Amen.
>
> (Luke 24:47-53)

> These all continued with one accord in prayer and
> supplication, with the women, and Mary the mother of
> Jesus, and with his brethren.
>
> (Acts 1:14)

The apostles returned to Jerusalem to the Upper Room where they continued in prayer and waited for the promise of the Father as Jesus said they would receive.

Acts chapter 1 tells us the actions of the apostles during the remainder of the day after the ascension and they returned to the Upper Room.

This was forty days after the resurrection of Jesus, now looking at Acts chapter 2, we are ten days later or fifty days after Jesus' resurrection (ten days after He ascended).

This was the day of Pentecost remember Jesus rose on Feast of Firstfruits.

> Which also said, Ye men of Galilee, why stand ye gazing
> up into heaven? this same Jesus, which is taken up from
> you into heaven, shall so come in like manner as ye have
> seen him go into heaven.
>
> (Acts 1:11)

> And ye shall count unto you from the morrow after the
> sabbath, from the day that ye brought the sheaf of the wave
> offering; seven sabbaths shall be complete:
> Even unto the morrow after the seventh sabbath shall
> ye number fifty days; and ye shall offer a new meat offering
> unto the LORD.
>
> (Leviticus 23:15-16)

Sometimes Pentecost is called the Festival of Weeks.

Pentecost the Day the Church Begin

He saith unto them, But whom say ye that I am?

And Simon Peter answered and said, Thou art the Christ, the Son of the living God.

And Jesus answered and said unto him, Blessed art thou, Simon Barjona: for flesh and blood hath not revealed it unto thee, but my Father which is in heaven.

And I say also unto thee, That thou art Peter, and upon this rock

I will build my church; and the gates of hell shall not prevail against it.

(Matthew 16:15-18)

(Greek Word: Πέτρος Transliteration: Petros, a pebble or small stone).
(Greek Word: πέτρα Transliteration: petra, a massive rock).

Who is the ROCK Peter or Jesus?

We have to go back to the Greek, the language in which the New Testament was written. There are two different meanings for rock. When Jesus gave Simon Barjona the name of Peter meaning rock it was *Petros*, a small pebble. The word rock used in Matthew 16:18 is *Petra*, a massive rock. The original wording reveals the true meaning of what is being said. Peter was correct when he stated Jesus was "the Christ" and upon this profession of truth would the church be founded. Jesus is the "chief cornerstone" or The ROCK. There is no other foundation on which the church can be laid.

And are built upon the foundation of the apostles and prophets, Jesus Christ himself being the chief corner stone;

(Ephesians 2:20)

Wherefore also it is contained in the scripture, Behold, I lay in Sion a chief corner stone, elect, precious: and he that believeth on him shall not be confounded.

(1 Peter 2:6)

The Promise of the Father
Apostles filled with the Holy Spirit

And when the day of Pentecost was fully come, <u>they</u> (the apostles) were all with one accord in one place.

And suddenly there came a sound from heaven as of a rushing mighty wind, and it filled all the house (Greek word for house *oikos*… meaning house or temple).

where <u>they</u> (the apostles) were sitting.

And there appeared unto <u>them</u> (the apostles) cloven tongues like as of fire, and it sat upon each of <u>them</u> (the apostles).

And <u>they</u> (the apostles) were all filled with the Holy Ghost, and began to speak with other tongues, as the Spirit gave <u>them</u> (the apostles) utterance.

(Acts 2:1-4; my emphasis)

Now the apostles were Jews and being devout men of God, they was required to be in the temple for the hour of prayer. There were three hours of prayer.

1. 9:00 am 3rd hour of the day
2. 3:00 pm 9th hour of the day
3. 6:00 pm 12th hour sundown

The apostles were in the temple praising God at 9:00 am or the third hour of their Jewish day.

While praising God all of a sudden they were filled with the Holy Ghost as Jesus promised they would be. This was exactly ten days after Jesus ascended to heaven to sit at the Father's right hand and be our high priest and intercessor in heaven. The Holy Spirit was the promise of the Father.

Peter is telling the men in the temple these men with me are not drunk, this is what the prophet Joel prophesied about. This is only the <u>third hour of the day.</u>

But Peter, standing up with the <u>eleven</u>, (not the hundred and twenty) lifted up his voice, and said unto them, Ye men of Judaea, and all ye that dwell at Jerusalem, be this known unto you, and hearken to my words:

For these are not drunken, as ye suppose, seeing it is <u>but the third hour of the day.</u>

(Acts 2:14-15; my emphasis)

Continue to read Acts 2 as it gives the message of Peter remembering that upon this profession of truth would the church be founded.

On this day there were 3,000 souls saved, this was the birth of the church. Pentecost was a pilgrim feast that meant according to God's Law, all adult Jewish men would come from wherever they were living to Jerusalem and attend the celebration. There were thousands and thousands in Jerusalem on this day and they were in the temple praising God.

<u>And they, continuing daily with one accord in the temple,</u> and breaking bread from house to house, did eat their meat with gladness and singleness of heart,

Praising God, and having favour with all the people. And the Lord added to the church daily such as should be saved.

(Acts 2:46-47)

Chapter 7

JESUS RETURNS

THE RAPTURE - JESUS WILL RETURN FOR HIS BRIDE

For the Lord himself shall descend from heaven with a
shout, with the voice of the archangel, and with the trump
of God: and the dead in Christ shall rise first:

Then we which are alive and remain shall be caught
up together with them in the clouds, to meet the Lord in
the air: and so shall we ever be with the Lord.

Wherefore comfort one another with these words.

(1 Thessalonians 4:16-18)

The trumpet call, not to be confused with the last of the seven trumpets in
Revelation, is a trumpet call associated with the Jewish Feast of Trumpets.
The dead in Christ shall rise first then we who are alive "caught up" to meet
the Lord in the air. Jesus returns for His bride (the church) before God
pours out His wrath upon the world (tribulation period).

The church is the bride of Christ, God intends that she join her bridegroom
for a great wedding feast and after that share with Him in ruling the

nations. God will not allow the church to suffer through the tribulation. He has called out the church from the world, He will rescued her "from the coming wrath." (1 Thessalonians 1:10)

> And to wait for his Son from heaven, whom he raised from the dead, even Jesus, which delivered us from the wrath to come.
>
> (1 Thessalonians 1:10)

> But of the times and the seasons, brethren, ye have no need that I write unto you.
>
> For yourselves know perfectly that the day of the Lord so cometh as a thief in the night.
>
> For when they shall say, Peace and safety; then sudden destruction cometh upon them, as travail upon a woman with child; and they shall not escape.
>
> But ye, brethren, are not in darkness, that that day should overtake you as a thief.
>
> Ye are all the children of light, and the children of the day: we are not of the night, nor of darkness.
>
> Therefore let us not sleep, as do others; but let us watch and be sober.
>
> For they that sleep sleep in the night; and they that be drunken are drunken in the night.
>
> But let us, who are of the day, be sober, putting on the breastplate of faith and love; and for an helmet, the hope of salvation.
>
> For God hath not appointed us to wrath, but to obtain salvation by our Lord Jesus Christ,
>
> Who died for us, that, whether we wake or sleep, we should live together with him.
>
> (1 Thessalonians 5:1-10)

> Behold, I shew you a mystery; We shall not all sleep, but we shall all be changed,
>
> In a moment, in the twinkling of an eye, at the last trump: for the trumpet shall sound, and the dead shall be raised incorruptible, and we shall be changed.
>
> (1 Corinthians 15:51-52)

The appointed times of the Lord's are like annual rehearsals and blueprints for the work of the Messiah. The spring festivals of Passover, Unleavened Bread, the First Fruits, and Pentecost all received a messianic fulfillment in the Master's first advent. The fall feasts of the Feast of Trumpets, the Day of Atonement, and the Feast of Tabernacles all point toward His second coming. They are a "shadow of what is to come."

Each of the "moadim" (the appointed times on the Holy Day calendar) are intended to reveal the framework of God's plan of redemption for man. If you have not studied the Feasts of the Lord's you are missing out on having a deeper understanding of God's plan for man. I hate to say this but the "church" has done a great injustice to the people by not teaching about these feasts.

There are seven feasts: feasts means Moadim or appointments and convocations are rehearsals.

In Leviticus 23:2 Yehovah tells us, "These are My appointed festivals, the appointed festivals of the Lord, which you are to proclaim as sacred assemblies." They are Yehovah's appointed times available to all His followers. Mark your calendar and plan ahead to participate with Yehovah on His Holy Days! *The three fall feasts are yet to be fulfilled*

1. Passover   Jesus fulfilled with his death on the cross
2. Feast of Unleavened Breads   Jesus fulfilled with his burial
3. Feast of First Fruits   Jesus rose from the grave
4. Feast of Weeks (Pentecost)   God sent the Holy Spirit

The above four feasts were fulfilled by Jesus on their exact day, they are the spring feasts.

5. Feast of Trumpets (Rosh Hashanah)
6. Day of Atonement
7. Feast of Tabernacles

The King is Coming

The return of Jesus has been debated with much speculation and controversy, is He coming back?

> Which also said, Ye men of Galilee, why stand ye gazing up into heaven? this same Jesus, which is taken up from you into heaven, shall so come in like manner as ye have seen him go into heaven.
>
> (Acts 1:11)

> But I would not have you to be ignorant, brethren, concerning them which are asleep, that ye sorrow not, even as others which have no hope.
>
> For if we believe that Jesus died and rose again, even so them also which sleep in Jesus will God bring with him.
>
> For this we say unto you by the word of the Lord, that we which are alive *and* remain unto the coming of the Lord shall not prevent them which are asleep.
>
> For the Lord himself shall descend from heaven with a shout, with the voice of the archangel, and with the trump of God: and the dead in Christ shall rise first:
>
> Then we which are alive *and* remain shall be caught up together with them in the clouds, to meet the Lord in the air: and so shall we ever be with the Lord.
>
> Wherefore comfort one another with these words.
>
> (1 Thessalonians 4:13-18)

Jesus is returning for His own, those who believe in Him and obey Him, He will receive unto Himself. I believe there are two separate events in the return of Jesus...

1. The Rapture – His coming in the air to catch away His bride (*The Church*).
2. The Second Coming – His return to earth.

THE RAPTURE — IN THE AIR

Jesus will come in the clouds and we will meet Him in the air to be ever with Him. It will be instant, in the twinkling of an eye and remove believers from the earth before the Great Tribulation (God's wrath).

> For the Lord himself shall descend from heaven with a shout, with the voice of the archangel, and with the trump of God: and the dead in Christ shall rise first:
> Then we which are alive *and* remain shall be caught up together with them in the clouds, to meet the Lord in the air: and so shall we ever be with the Lord.
> (1 Thessalonians 4:16-17)

> Now this I say, brethren, that flesh and blood cannot inherit the kingdom of God; neither doth corruption inherit incorruption.
> Behold, I shew you a mystery; We shall not all sleep, but we shall all be changed,
> <u>In a moment, in the twinkling of an eye,</u> at the **last trump***: for the trumpet shall sound, and the dead shall be raised incorruptible, and we shall be changed.
> (1 Corinthians 15:50-52)

* Paul was one of the greatest apostles, he understood the Old Covenant much better than most Christians know and understand the New Covenant. He sat and learned at the feet of Gamaliel, one of the greatest scholars of the Old Testament. Paul understood "God's feasts". During the feasts, shofars were blown at certain times. The understanding of these feasts include the timing and the specific patterns of the sounds and the lengths of these sounds. For instance, let's use the pattern in use for the Fall Feast of Trumpets: Please understand that the pattern will include each of four sounds of the shofar).

1. This sound is called Tekiah—a "blast" of the trumpet—meaning to "wake up!", or "be alert!"

2. This sound is called Sh'varim—"short blasts" to be broken, humbled, ordered repentance.
3. This sound is called T'ruah—"Repeated short blasts"; an alarm; Get prepared!
4. This sound is called Tekiah Gedolah—"long tone", it's the Last Trump. Denotes hope of redemption.

The Last Trump is the fourth sound—the last sound of a pattern of shofar sounds—the Resurrection/Rapture.

There are those that believe Paul is referring to the seventh trumpet in Revelation, however Paul was writing to the Corinthians and his letter was composed about AD 55.

The book of Revelation which talks about the seven trumpets during the great tribulation, was written by John, the apostle, around AD 95-96. So the Corinthians would have had no knowledge of the seven trumpets talked about in Revelation, but they would know about the **last trump** blown on the Feasts of Trumpets (Rosh Hashanah). The Bible talks about many trumpets but nowhere in Revelation does it mention *"the last trump"*.

> For God hath not appointed us to wrath, but to obtain salvation by our Lord Jesus Christ,
> Who died for us, that, whether we wake or sleep, we should live together with him.
> (1 Thessalonians 5:9-10)

> Because thou hast kept the word of my patience, <u>I also will keep thee from the hour of temptation,</u> which shall come upon all the world, to try them that dwell upon the earth.
> (Revelation 3:10)

The believers (bride of Christ) that are raptured will be judged individually for their deeds on earth. They will receive their rewards at the Bema Seat Judgement and the Lord Himself will judge the works of the redeemed not for good or evil, but to determine motive and character. The believer will either receive a reward or lose a reward.

The believers sins have been covered by the blood of Jesus, they are gone, no more to be remembered once you except Jesus as your savior and continue to live for Him; I believe you can walk away from God, but God will not leave you. It is your works that Jesus is testing here at the Bema Seat Judgement and rewards will be given or lost. Your works does not save you but they are what your rewards are based on. You must believe on Jesus and accept Him as your savior in order to be in the bride of Christ *(the Church)*.

> For we must all appear before the judgment seat of Christ; that every one may receive the things *done* in *his* body, according to that he hath done, whether *it be* good or bad.
>
> (2 Corinthians 5:10)

> Every man's work shall be made manifest: for the day shall declare it, because it shall be revealed by fire; and the fire shall try every man's work of what sort it is.
>
> If any man's work abide which he hath built thereupon, he shall receive a reward.
>
> If any man's work shall be burned, he shall suffer loss: but he himself shall be saved; yet so as by fire.
>
> (1 Corinthians 3:13-15)

CROWNS TO BE AWARDED

1. The *incorruptible crown*: to be given to believers who faithfully run the race, who crucify every selfish desire in order to win souls and point men to Jesus.

> Know ye not that they which run in a race run all, but one receiveth the prize? So run, that ye may obtain.
>
> And every man that striveth for the mastery is temperate in all things. Now they *do it* to obtain a corruptible crown; but we an incorruptible.
>
> (1 Corinthians 9:24-25)

2. The *crown of rejoicing:* soul-winner's crown, and it may be earned by every born again believer who faithfully witnesses to the saving grace of God and leads souls to Jesus.

> For what *is* our hope, or joy, or crown of rejoicing? *Are* not even ye in the presence of our Lord Jesus Christ at his coming? For ye are our glory and joy.
>
> (1 Thessalonians 2:19-20)

3. The *crown of life:* crown is for those believers who endure trials, tribulations, and severe suffering-yes, even unto death

> Blessed *is* the man that endureth temptation: for when he is tried, he shall receive the crown of life, which the Lord hath promised to them that love him.
>
> (James 1:12)

4. The *crown of righteousness:* crown is for believers who love the appearing of Christ, who anxiously wait and look forward to the day when He will return for His saints.

> Henceforth there is laid up for me a crown of righteousness, which the Lord, the righteous judge, shall give me at that day: and not to me only, but unto all them also that love his appearing.
>
> (2 Timothy 4:8)

5. The *crown of glory:* This is the pastor's crown and will be given to the ministers who are faithful and feed the lock of God.

> Feed the flock of God which is among you, taking the oversight *thereof,* not by constraint, but willingly; not for filthy lucre, but of a ready mind;
> Neither as being lords over *God's* heritage, but being ensamples to the flock.
> And when the chief Shepherd shall appear, ye shall receive a crown of glory that fadeth not away.
>
> (1 Peter 5:2-4)

THE MARRIAGE SUPPER OF THE LAMB

The scriptures tell us that the Church is the bride of Christ, so that makes Jesus Christ the bridegroom. The marriage in Old Testament times were arranged by the parents. In the marriage of the Lamb, the Father chose the Bride for His Son. To fully understand the "marriage made in heaven" we need to understand the Jewish wedding. (see Chapter 8 "Marriage Made in Heaven" on the Jewish Wedding).

WHEN JESUS RETURNS TO EARTH -THE SECOND COMING

The disciples ask Jesus for the sign of the <u>end of the world</u>. Remember the disciples had no clue or knowledge concerning the church. So in Matthew 24 Jesus is telling them concerning His second coming, it does not pertain to the rapture. The church did not exist until the book of Acts and Paul is the one that reveals the *mystery of the church* in his teachings in (I Corinthians 15:50-51).

Jesus was very specific in describing signs and the end of the world, He talks about the "abomination of desolation" in the temple that was prophesied by Daniel. The temple was destroyed in AD 70, therefore a new temple will be rebuilt in God's timing.

I ask the question, "Why a new temple and animal sacrifices again"? Jesus dies for our sins, He is the one and only sacrifice now. Remember the Jews were offering sacrifices during the time Jesus was living before He was crucified, they did not believe Jesus as their Messiah, because of unbelief Israel was cut off as a nation and the birth of the church as seen in Acts began. Is God finished with Israel? NO. Once the church has been raptured God will turn back to Israel and deal with her, they will pick up where they left off and sacrifices will once again be offered in the new temple.

There is an organization in Israel called the Temple Institute, founded in 1987 to educate and organize the rebuilding of the holy temple. They have already begun to construct the sacred vessels that will be ready for service in the new temple.

> And as he sat upon the mount of Olives, the disciples came unto him privately, saying, Tell us, when shall these things be? and what *shall be* the sign of thy coming, and of the end of the world?
>
> (Matthew 24:3)

Revelation chapters 6-19 tells us what takes place during the Great Tribulation and the Church is never mentioned in these chapters.

> And Enoch also, the seventh from Adam, prophesied of these, saying, Behold, the Lord cometh with ten thousands of his saints,
>
> To execute judgment upon all, and to convince all that are ungodly among them of all their ungodly deeds which they have ungodly committed, and of all their hard *speeches* which ungodly sinners have spoken against him.
>
> (Jude 1:14-15)

> Behold, he cometh with clouds; and every eye shall see him, and they *also* which pierced him: and all kindreds of the earth shall wail because of him. Even so, Amen.
>
> (Revelation 1:7)

> And I saw heaven opened, and behold a white horse; and he that sat upon him *was* called Faithful and True, and in righteousness he doth judge and make war.
>
> His eyes *were* as a flame of fire, and on his head *were* many crowns; and he had a name written, that no man knew, but he himself.
>
> And he *was* clothed with a vesture dipped in blood: and his name is called The Word of God.
>
> And the armies *which were* in heaven followed him upon white horses, clothed in fine linen, white and clean.
>
> (Revelation 19:11-14)

Jesus will return to smite the nations that have opposed Him, the beast and false prophet will be thrown into the lake of fire, and Satan will be bound a thousand years. Jesus will rule and reign in the millennial kingdom after the tribulation; there will be souls saved out of the tribulation period and taken to heaven and there will be people that live and make it through the tribulation period. There will be a judgement of the sheep and goat nations and the sheep will enter into the millennial kingdom for a thousand year reign with Jesus.

> And before him shall be gathered all nations: and he shall separate them one from another, as a shepherd divideth *his* sheep from the goats:
> And he shall set the sheep on his right hand, but the goats on the left.
> Then shall the King say unto them on his right hand, Come, ye blessed of my Father, inherit the kingdom prepared for you from the foundation of the world:
> (Matthew 25:32-34)

The raptured saints and the tribulation saints will rule and reign with Jesus during the thousand years over the people that survive the tribulation period and make it into the millennial kingdom. The survivors of the tribulation period will be in their natural bodies; even with Satan bound during the millennium people will still sin, people are still in their flesh and flesh will be tripping people up, yet it will be a peaceful reign with Jesus at the helm. People will live as we do today, marrying and giving birth, thousands will be born during the millennial reign, but it will be a peaceful period. The animals will be tame like they were before the flood. The Bible tells us that the Lamb will lie down with the Lion.

ISAIAH PROPHESIZES OF THE PEACEFUL KINGDOM

> And there shall come forth a rod out of the stem of Jesse, and a Branch shall grow out of his roots:
> And the spirit of the LORD shall rest upon him, the spirit of wisdom and understanding, the spirit of counsel

and might, the spirit of knowledge and of the fear of the LORD;

And shall make him of quick understanding in the fear of the LORD: and he shall not judge after the sight of his eyes, neither reprove after the hearing of his ears:

But with righteousness shall he judge the poor, and reprove with equity for the meek of the earth: and he shall smite the earth with the rod of his mouth, and with the breath of his lips shall he slay the wicked.

And righteousness shall be the girdle of his loins, and faithfulness the girdle of his reins.

The wolf also shall dwell with the lamb, and the leopard shall lie down with the kid; and the calf and the young lion and the fatling together; and a little child shall lead them.

And the cow and the bear shall feed; their young ones shall lie down together: and the lion shall eat straw like the ox.

And the sucking child shall play on the hole of the asp, and the weaned child shall put his hand on the cockatrice' den.

They shall not hurt nor destroy in all my holy mountain: for the earth shall be full of the knowledge of the LORD, as the waters cover the sea.

(Isaiah 11:1-9)

And I saw thrones, and they sat upon them, and judgment was given unto them: and I saw the souls of them that were beheaded for the witness of Jesus, and for the word of God, and which had not worshipped the beast, neither his image, neither had received his mark upon their foreheads, or in their hands; and they lived and reigned with Christ a thousand years.

But the rest of the dead lived not again until the thousand years were finished. This is the first resurrection.

Blessed and holy is he that hath part in the first resurrection: on such the second death hath no power, but they shall be priests of God and of Christ, and shall reign with him a thousand years.

(Revelation 20:4-6)

After the thousand years Satan will be loosed and will once again be free to tempt people…some will be true to Jesus and some will follow Satan.

There will be a final battle where Satan will be defeated and Jesus Christ will triumph.

This will be short-lived war and Satan and his followers will be cast into the Lake of Fire

And when the thousand years are expired, Satan shall be loosed out of his prison,

(Revelation 20:7)

And they went up on the breadth of the earth, and compassed the camp of the saints about, and the beloved city: and fire came down from God out of heaven, and devoured them.

And the devil that deceived them was cast into the lake of fire and brimstone, where the beast and the false prophet *are*, and shall be tormented day and night for ever and ever.

(Revelation 20:9-10)

And the angels which kept not their first estate, but left their own habitation, he hath reserved in everlasting chains under darkness unto the judgment of the great day.

Even as Sodom and Gomorrha, and the cities about them in like manner, giving themselves over to fornication, and going after strange flesh, are set forth for an example, suffering the vengeance of eternal fire.

(Jude 1:6-7)

The Great White Throne Judgement is the final judgement and all the unsaved people will be judged and thrown into the Lake of Fire this is the second death.

And I saw the dead, small and great, stand before God; and the books were opened: and another book was opened, which is *the book* of life: and the dead were judged out of those things which were written in the books, according to their works.

(Revelation 20:12)

THE NEW EARTH AND THE NEW JERUSALEM

For the Father judgeth no man, but hath committed all judgment unto the Son:

Heaven and earth will pass away and a New heaven and earth will come down from God out of heaven and Jesus Christ will reign forever more.

(John 5:22)

And I saw a new heaven and a new earth: for the first heaven and the first earth were passed away; and there was no more sea.

And I John saw the holy city, new Jerusalem, coming down from God out of heaven, prepared as a bride adorned for her husband.

And I heard a great voice out of heaven saying, Behold, the tabernacle of God *is* with men, and he will dwell with them, and they shall be his people, and God himself shall be with them, *and be* their God.

And God shall wipe away all tears from their eyes; and there shall be no more death, neither sorrow, nor crying, neither shall there be any more pain: for the former things are passed away.

And he that sat upon the throne said, Behold, I make all things new. And he said unto me, Write: for these words are true and faithful.

And he said unto me, It is done. I am Alpha and Omega, the beginning and the end. I will give unto him that is athirst of the fountain of the water of life freely.

He that overcometh shall inherit all things; and I will
be his God, and he shall be my son.

But the fearful, and unbelieving, and the abominable,
and murderers, and whoremongers, and sorcerers, and
idolaters, and all liars, shall have their part in the lake
which burneth with fire and brimstone: which is the
second death.

(Revelation 21:1-8)

The saints will live forevermore in the new earth and New Jerusalem that
God has prepared for all followers of Jesus. The new heaven and new earth
will be "where righteousness dwells". After the re-creation, God reveals the
New Jerusalem, John sees a glimpse of it in his vision: "The Holy City, the
New Jerusalem, coming down from God out of heaven, prepared as a bride
beautifully dressed for her husband". This is the city that Abraham looked
for in faith. It is the place where God will dwell with His people forever;
inhabitants of this celestial city will have all tears wiped away.

The New Jerusalem will be huge. John records that the city is 1,400 miles
long, and it is as wide and as high as it is long—a perfect cube. The city
will be beyond our imagination in every way. It is lighted by the glory of
God. Its twelve foundations, bearing the names of the twelve apostles, are
decorated with every kind of precious stone. It has twelve gates of a single
pearl, bearing the names of the twelve tribes of Israel. The streets are made
of pure gold.

The curse of the old earth will be gone and in the city are the tree of life
"for the healing of the nations" and the river of life. The New Jerusalem
is God's goodness made fully manifest. What God has prepared for us is
beyond our imagination or any description. I can't begin to imagine the
beauty and wonder of what we will behold in heaven.

Chapter 8

A MARRIAGE MADE IN HEAVEN

God the Father, Jesus the Son, and the Bride (The Church)

Jesus being a Jew used many illustrations in His teaching that the Jews could easily relate too;

One of these was the Jewish wedding ceremony and how He compared it to the Bride of Christ and His return to gather His church.

There are several parts to the Jewish wedding and I will attempt to explain them as they relate to our Christian life.

THE CONTRACT OR DOCUMENT

The first part of the Jewish wedding ceremony was the *betrothal*, which was called the *kiddashin*. The marriage of a daughter was arranged by her parents, they would come together with the young man and make an agreement. A marriage contract was drawn up and in it he would list all of the things he had to offer the girl. There was a cup of wine that both the young man and the young women would partake of, if she agreed to the arrangement. The agreement would be sealed by a ring or a document, which was symbolic of a promise providing a legal tie between the two.

God has given us a **document** (the Bible) listing all the things He has to offer us and what is in store for those who abide by His rules.

THE MOHAR OR BRIDE PRICE

This was required by law and paid by the father of the groom, showing the value of the bride.

God the Father paid the price of giving His only Son as a sacrifice for our sins.

> For what the law could not do, in that it was weak through the flesh, God sending his own Son in the likeness of sinful flesh, and for sin, condemned sin in the flesh:
> That the righteousness of the law might be fulfilled in us, who walk not after the flesh, but after the Spirit.
> (Romans 8:3-4)

> For ye are bought with a price: therefore glorify God in your body, and in your spirit, which are God's.
> (1 Corinthians 6:20)

> Forasmuch as ye know that ye were not redeemed with corruptible things, *as* silver and gold, from your vain conversation *received* by tradition from your fathers;
> But with the precious blood of Christ, as of a lamb without blemish and without spot:
> (1 Peter 1:18-19)

> For God so loved the world, that he gave his only begotten Son, that whosoever believeth in him should not perish, but have everlasting life.
> (John 3:16)

The Mattan or Love Gifts

The groom would present love gifts to the bride to be, but this was not required.

Jesus presents to us many gifts of love of which three are...there are many more.

1. Eternal Life
2. Anything asked in Jesus name
3. Peace

> My sheep hear my voice, and I know them, and they follow me:
>> And I give unto them eternal life; and they shall never perish, neither shall any *man* pluck them out of my hand.
>> (John 10:27-28)

> And whatsoever ye shall ask in my name, that will I do, that the Father may be glorified in the Son.
>> If ye shall ask any thing in my name, I will do *it*.
>> (John 14:13-14)

> Peace I leave with you, my peace I give unto you: not as the world giveth, give I unto you. Let not your heart be troubled, neither let it be afraid.
>> (John 14:27)

The Shiluhim — Dowry

The father of the bride would give to her a dowry which was part of her inheritance.

God has provided us with many gifts to equip us for a new life in Jesus Christ as we live our life for Him.

- The Holy Spirit
- Spiritual Gifts

And I will pray the Father, and he shall give you another Comforter, that he may abide with you for ever;

Even the Spirit of truth; whom the world cannot receive, because it seeth him not, neither knoweth him: but ye know him; for he dwelleth with you, and shall be in you.

(John 14:16-17)

Now he which stablisheth us with you in Christ, and hath anointed us, *is* God;

Who hath also sealed us, and given the earnest of the Spirit in our hearts.

(2 Corinthians 1:21-22)

Blessed *be* the God and Father of our Lord Jesus Christ, who hath blessed us with all spiritual blessings in heavenly *places* in Christ:

According as he hath chosen us in him before the foundation of the world, that we should be holy and without blame before him in love:

Having predestinated us unto the adoption of children by Jesus Christ to himself, according to the good pleasure of his will,

To the praise of the glory of his grace, wherein he hath made us accepted in the beloved.

In whom we have redemption through his blood, the forgiveness of sins, according to the riches of his grace;

Wherein he hath abounded toward us in all wisdom and prudence;

Having made known unto us the mystery of his will, according to his good pleasure which he hath purposed in himself:

That in the dispensation of the fulness of times he might gather together in one all things in Christ, both which are in heaven, and which are on earth; *even* in him:

In whom also we have obtained an **inheritance**, being predestinated according to the purpose of him who worketh all things after the counsel of his own will:

That we should be to the praise of his glory, who first trusted in Christ.

In whom ye also *trusted*, after that ye heard the word of truth, the gospel of your salvation: in whom also after that ye believed, ye were sealed with that **holy Spirit of promise,**

Which is the earnest of our **inheritance** until the redemption of the purchased possession, unto the praise of his glory.

(Ephesians 1:3-14)

KETUBAH — THE MARRIAGE CONTRACT

The Mohar, written document stating the Rights of the bride and the promises of the groom

The Bible, our document, God's written Word has many, many promises as we live a life for Jesus Christ.

For all the promises of God in him *are* yea, and in him Amen, unto the glory of God by us.

(2 Corinthians 1:20)

For I know the thoughts that I think toward you, saith the LORD, thoughts of peace, and not of evil, to give you an expected end.

(Jeremiah 29: 11)

Come unto me, all *ye* that labour and are heavy laden, and I will give you rest.

Take my yoke upon you, and learn of me; for I am meek and lowly in heart: and ye shall find rest unto your souls.

(Matthew 11:28-29)

But my God shall supply all your need according to his riches in glory by Christ Jesus.

(Philippians 4:19)

But now hath he obtained a more excellent ministry, by how much also he is the mediator of a better covenant, which was established upon better promises.

(Hebrews 8:6)

KIDDUSHIN — THE BETROTHAL

The word "kiddushin" comes from the <u>root</u> Qof-Dalet-Shin, meaning "sanctified."

Kiddushin is far more binding than an engagement as we understand the term in today's world. Once kiddushin is complete, the woman is legally the wife of the man. The relationship created by kiddushin can only be dissolved by death or divorce. However, the spouses do not live together until the nisuin (the actual wedding ceremony) is complete.

- Purification (Mikveh)... *The **mikveh** is a ritual bath designed for the Jewish rite of **purification**.*
- Undistracted devotion... *although they do not live together they are devoted to each other.*
- Sealed with a cup of wine... *acceptance*

God has made a new covenant with man, Jesus Christ is the price that was paid and we are to be his if we accept this covenant.

- Cup of the New Covenant
- Christ goes to prepare a place for us
- We are 'set apart' "sanctified"
- Purified by 'washing of the Word'

And as they were eating, Jesus took bread, and blessed *it*, and brake *it*, and gave *it* to the disciples, and said, Take, eat; this is my body.

And he took the cup, and gave thanks, and gave *it* to them, saying, Drink ye all of it;

For this is my blood of the new testament, which is shed for many for the remission of sins.

But I say unto you, I will not drink henceforth of this fruit of the vine, until that day when I drink it new with you in my Father's kingdom.

(Matthew 26:26-29)

Let not your heart be troubled: ye believe in God, believe also in me.

In my Father's house are many mansions: if *it were* not *so*, I would have told you. I go to prepare a place for you.

And if I go and prepare a place for you, I will come again, and receive you unto myself; that where I am, *there* ye may be also.

(John 14:1-3)

For I am jealous over you with godly jealousy: for I have espoused you to one husband, that I may present *you as* a chaste virgin to Christ.

(2 Corinthians 11:2)

And such were some of you: but ye are washed, but ye are sanctified, but ye are justified in the name of the Lord Jesus, and by the Spirit of our God.

(1 Corinthians 6:11)

When the Lord returns we will drink of the final cup of wine to celebrate the wedding ceremony of the church and Jesus Christ.

For I say unto you, I will not any more eat thereof, until it be fulfilled in the kingdom of God.

And he took the cup, and gave thanks, and said, Take this, and divide *it* among yourselves:

For I say unto you, I will not drink of the fruit of the vine, until the kingdom of God shall come.

(Luke 22:16-18)

Jesus will return for His Bride... Jesus said where I am ye may be also.

He will come again in the clouds to gather His Bride to Himself, <u>then will return with His bride</u> and a host of angels to rule and reign. This is His second coming to *earth*.

Chapter 9

GOD'S SPECIAL DAYS

GOD'S FEASTS OR APPOINTED TIMES
ALSO CALLED "HOLY CONVOCATIONS"

We all enjoy and love our holidays, I love family gatherings, especially at Thanksgiving and Christmas, but Israel is the only nation that has had their holidays appointed by God. **The Jewish holy days *(holidays)* are not only historic... but prophetic and very definitely point to Israel's Messiah.** There is a crimson thread that connect these "rehearsal" days.

God's seven feasts are an outline of God's redemptive plan. They are <u>"Appointed Times" of meeting with God and represent foreshadowing events of 'God's plan'</u>. They are rehearsals for future events in God's time table. The first four feasts, Passover, Unleavened Bread, First Fruits and Feast of Weeks foreshadowed prophetic events of Jesus' first coming. The last three feasts, Trumpets, Atonement, and Tabernacles foreshadow Jesus' return at the 'End of Time'.

God's feasts are for us to remember what has happened and what is to come.

- <u>Remembrance</u> = deliverance from bondage.
- <u>Thanksgiving</u> = Fulfillment of Redemptive promises / prophecies.
- <u>Anticipation</u> = His future deliverance and communion with God.

And the LORD spake unto Moses, saying,
Speak unto the children of Israel, and say unto them, *Concerning* the feasts of the LORD, which ye shall proclaim *to be* holy convocations, *even* these *are* my feasts.
Six days shall work be done: but the seventh day *is* the sabbath of rest, an holy convocation; ye shall do no work *therein*: it *is* the sabbath of the LORD in all your dwellings.
These *are* the feasts of the LORD, *even* holy convocations, which ye shall proclaim in their seasons.
(Leviticus 23:1-4)

Let no man therefore judge you in meat, or in drink, or in respect of an holyday, or of the new moon, or of the sabbath *days*:
Which are a <u>shadow of things to come</u>; but the body *is* of Christ.
(Colossians 2:16-17)

God gave Moses the dates and how to observe these seven feasts while at Mount Sinai and following are their names.

Spring Feasts...

1. Passover (Pesach) – Nisan 14 Jesus Crucifixion
2. Unleavened Bread (Chag Hamotzi) – Nisan 15-22 Jesus Burial
3. First Fruits a(Yom habikkurim) – Nisan 16-17 Jesus Resurrection

Summer Feasts...

4. Pentecost (Shavu'ot) - Sivan 6-7 Gift of the Holy Spirit

Fall Feasts...

5. Trumpets (Yom Teru'ah) – Tishri 1

6. Atonement (Yom Kippur) – Tishri 10
7. Tabernacles (Sukkot) – Tishri 15-22

All the spring and summer feasts have been fulfilled by Jesus and the fall feasts will be fulfilled at God's appointed times. Celebrating the feasts each year was and is a rehearsal for what was fulfilled and what will be fulfilled in the future by the Fall Feasts.

Passover – (Not a Sabbath, but a day of preparation for a High Sabbath). Salvation is by the atoning blood of the promised sacrificed lamb.

This was the fulfillment of Passover for Israel's national salvation, deliverance from the bondage of Egypt; the Blood Covenant for redemption of mankind and the only way of salvation. There is no other way of salvation. Jeremiah spoke of this 600 years before Jesus died on the cross, a shadow of things to come.

> Behold, the days come, saith the LORD, that I will make a new covenant with the house of Israel, and with the house of Judah:
> Not according to the covenant that I made with their fathers in the day *that* I took them by the hand to bring them out of the land of Egypt; which my covenant they brake, although I was an husband unto them, saith the LORD:
> But this *shall be* the covenant that I will make with the house of Israel; After those days, saith the LORD, I will put my law in their inward parts, and write it in their hearts; and will be their God, and they shall be my people.
> (Jeremiah 31:31-33)

> And the LORD spake unto Moses and Aaron in the land of Egypt, saying,
> This month *shall be* unto you the beginning of months: it *shall be* the first month of the year to you.
> Speak ye unto all the congregation of Israel, saying, In the tenth *day* of this month they shall take to them every

man a lamb, according to the house of *their* fathers, a lamb for an house:

And if the household be too little for the lamb, let him and his neighbour next unto his house take *it* according to the number of the souls; every man according to his eating shall make your count for the lamb.

Your lamb shall be without blemish, a male of the first year: ye shall take *it* out from the sheep, or from the goats:

And ye shall keep it up until the fourteenth day of the same month: and the whole assembly of the congregation of Israel shall kill it in the evening.

And they shall take of the blood, and strike *it* on the two side posts and on the upper door post of the houses, wherein they shall eat it.

And they shall eat the flesh in that night, roast with fire, and unleavened bread; *and* with bitter *herbs* they shall eat it.

Eat not of it raw, nor sodden at all with water, but roast *with* fire; his head with his legs, and with the purtenance thereof.

And ye shall let nothing of it remain until the morning; and that which remaineth of it until the morning ye shall burn with fire.

And thus shall ye eat it; *with* your loins girded, your shoes on your feet, and your staff in your hand; and ye shall eat it in haste: it *is* the LORD'S passover.

For I will pass through the land of Egypt this night, and will smite all the firstborn in the land of Egypt, both man and beast; and against all the gods of Egypt I will execute judgment: I *am* the LORD.

And the blood shall be to you for a token upon the houses where ye *are*: and when I see the blood, I will pass over you, and the plague shall not be upon you to destroy *you*, when I smite the land of Egypt.

And this day shall be unto you for a memorial; and ye shall keep it a feast to the LORD throughout your generations; ye shall keep it a feast by an ordinance for ever.

(Exodus 12:1-14)

> And the LORD spake unto Moses in the wilderness of Sinai, in the first month of the second year after they were come out of the land of Egypt, saying,
>
> Let the children of Israel also keep the passover at his appointed season.
>
> In the fourteenth day of this month, at even, ye shall keep it in his appointed season: according to all the rites of it, and according to all the ceremonies thereof, shall ye keep it.
>
> And Moses spake unto the children of Israel, that they should keep the passover.
>
> And they kept the passover on the fourteenth day of the first month at even in the wilderness of Sinai: according to all that the LORD commanded Moses, so did the children of Israel.
>
> (Numbers 9:1-5)

All the blood sacrifices going back to the Garden of Eden looked forward to a greater sacrifice, an ultimate sacrificial lamb who would give his sinless life for the world.

Abraham as he was preparing to give his son as a sacrifice said," God will provide Himself, a Lamb".

> And Abraham said, My son, God will provide himself a lamb for a burnt offering: so they went both of them together.
>
> (Genesis 22:8)

So on Palm Sunday Jesus made His entry into Jerusalem through the Eastern Gate and to the temple to be inspected by the Pharisees, the Sadducees, the Herodians, and the Scribes who sought to entrap Him. Just as the lamb was lead to the temple to be inspected before being sacrificed for the sins of Israel, Jesus was inspected and questioned, but they could find no fault in Him. No doubt some believed Jesus was the Messiah they had so long awaited, but it was not a majority. They all had access to the Torah (God's Word), they had studied the Torah, the learned priests of that day, (the Pharisees and Sadducees) did they not understand God's Word?

A perfect sacrifice, the Son of God would laid down His life for you and me, that we might have life through His atoning blood. Can we, or do we understand as we search the scripture, do we really search the scripture? Do we just read without understanding? I did for a long time, but the Word tells us to search diligently.

> Study to shew thyself approved unto God, a workman that needeth not to be ashamed, rightly dividing the word of truth.
>
> (2 Timothy 2:15)

from <u><G4710></u> (spoude); to *use speed*, i.e. to *make effort, be prompt* or *earnest* :- do (give) diligence, be diligent (forward), endeavour, labour, study. *Strong's Talking Greek & Hebrew Dictionary.*

> All scripture *is* given by inspiration of God, and *is* profitable for doctrine, for reproof, for correction, for instruction in righteousness:
> That the man of God may be perfect, thoroughly furnished unto all good works.
>
> (2 Timothy 3:16-17)

JESUS FULFILLED GOD'S APPOINTED TIME FOR PASSOVER

Passover service is commanded by Jesus Christ for His saints today, to observe, to remember every year to partake of its symbols, so as never to forget to understand its everlasting, spiritual meaning for life. Christ commands His church, "to observe this service for an ordinance, to thee and thy sons forever,"

Jesus Christ told His disciples…

> And as they were eating, Jesus took bread, and blessed *it*, and brake *it*, and gave *it* to the disciples, and said, Take, eat; this is my body.

And he took the cup, and gave thanks, and gave *it* to them, saying, Drink ye all of it;

For this is my blood of the new testament, which is shed for many for the remission of sins.

But I say unto you, I will not drink henceforth of this fruit of the vine, until that day when I drink it new with you in my Father's kingdom.

(Matthew 26:26-29)

And as they did eat, Jesus took bread, and blessed, and brake *it*, and gave to them, and said, Take, eat: this is my body.

And he took the cup, and when he had given thanks, he gave *it* to them: and they all drank of it.

And he said unto them, This is my blood of the new testament, which is shed for many.

Verily I say unto you, I will drink no more of the fruit of the vine, until that day that I drink it new in the kingdom of God.

(Mark 14:22-25)

And he took the cup, and gave thanks, and said, Take this, and divide *it* among yourselves:

For I say unto you, I will not drink of the fruit of the vine, until the kingdom of God shall come.

And he took bread, and gave thanks, and brake *it*, and gave unto them, saying, This is my body which is given for you: this do in remembrance of me.

Likewise also the cup after supper, saying, This cup *is* the new testament in my blood, which is shed for you.

(Luke 22:17-20)

Then Jesus said unto them, Verily, verily, I say unto you, Except ye eat the flesh of the Son of man, and drink his blood, ye have no life in you.

(John 6:53)

The Bible also says and warns us…

> For as often as ye eat this bread, and drink this cup, ye do shew the Lord's death till he come.
>
> Wherefore whosoever shall eat this bread, and drink *this* cup of the Lord, unworthily, shall be guilty of the body and blood of the Lord.
>
> But let a man examine himself, and so let him eat of *that* bread, and drink of *that* cup.
>
> For he that eateth and drinketh unworthily, eateth and drinketh damnation to himself, not discerning the Lord's body.
>
> For this cause many *are* weak and sickly among you, and many sleep.
>
> (1 Corinthians 11:26-30)

> For if we sin wilfully after that we have received the knowledge of the truth, there remaineth no more sacrifice for sins,
>
> But a certain fearful looking for of judgment and fiery indignation, which shall devour the adversaries.
>
> He that despised Moses' law died without mercy under two or three witnesses:
>
> Of how much sorer punishment, suppose ye, shall he be thought worthy, who hath trodden under foot the Son of God, and hath counted the blood of the covenant, wherewith he was sanctified, an unholy thing, and hath done despite unto the Spirit of grace?
>
> For we know him that hath said, Vengeance *belongeth* unto me, I will recompense, saith the Lord. And again, The Lord shall judge his people.
>
> *It is* a fearful thing to fall into the hands of the living God.
>
> (Hebrews 10:26-31)

Jesus died on Passover Nisan the 14th thus fulfilling God's appointed time or holy convocation.

THE FEAST OF UNLEAVENED BREAD

UNLEAVENED BREAD (*Chag HaMotzi*) (a High Sabbath - 7 day feast)

This feast day followed passover the very next day on the fifteenth of the same month. Leaven or yeast in the Bible symbolizes sin. When the children of Israel left Egypt they did not have time for their bread to rise, so they made it without leaven. When leaven is put into bread it permeates the entire loaf and courses it to rise. Leaven is symbolic of sin in the Bible, and when sin is permitted in a person's life it will eventually affect the whole body. This feast was to commemorate leaving Egypt in a hurry and grabbing the necessities and flee the land of bondage in Egypt. Today the Jews eat Matzoh, a bread made without yeast, and it has stripes that look like bruises and is pierced through, the holes are poked into the dough to keep it from being puffy and causes the hole lines to get slightly burnt in the oven thus looking like stripes. Unleavened Bread or Matzoh means cake without leaven.

> And on the fifteenth day of the same month *is* the feast of unleavened bread unto the LORD: seven days ye must eat unleavened bread.
>
> (Leviticus 23:6)

> Thou shalt eat no leavened bread with it; seven days shalt thou eat unleavened bread therewith, *even* the bread of affliction; for thou camest forth out of the land of Egypt in haste: that thou mayest remember the day when thou camest forth out of the land of Egypt all the days of thy life.
>
> (Deuteronomy 16:3)

> A little leaven leaveneth the whole lump.
>
> (Galatians 5:9)

In celebrating Passover (or Seder) the Jews today place 3 cakes of Matzoh in a bag, the middle matzoh is broken and wrapped in its own cloth and hidden somewhere in the house. Later the children are sent to find the hidden bread and return it to the father who promised to give them a prize.

Some say the three cakes symbolizes the three patriarchs, Abraham, Isaac, and Jacob – but the middle matzoh can't symbolize Isaac, since he was not broken, wrapped or hidden. The bread that was hidden was also called the afikoman.

> And he *(Jesus)* took bread, and gave thanks, and brake
> *it*, and gave unto them, saying, This is my body which is
> given for you: this do in remembrance of me.
>
> (Luke 22:19)

Just before sunset on Passover Jesus was buried, before the High Sabbath of Feast of Unleavened Bread. That Passover the sinless 'Bread of Heaven' became the perfect sacrifice for sin and He laid in a new tomb on the Feast of Unleavened Bread.

> Surely he hath borne our griefs, and carried our sorrows:
> yet we did esteem him stricken, smitten of God, and
> afflicted.
> But he *was* wounded for our transgressions, *he was*
> bruised for our iniquities: the chastisement of our peace
> *was* upon him; and with his stripes we are healed.
>
> (Isaiah 53:4-5)

Thus He fulfilled the Feast of Unleavened Bread.

THE FEAST OF FIRSTFRUITS

A work day following the weekly Sabbath that came after Passover. The Feast of Firstfruits was the barley harvest and had special meaning for the people of Israel as they gathered for God's appointed time. This celebration of waving of the first fruits of the barley harvest before God, in time would take on a deeper meaning to the Jewish people and to us as Christians.

> And the LORD spake unto Moses, saying,
> Speak unto the children of Israel, and say unto them,
> When ye be come into the land which I give unto you, and

shall reap the harvest thereof, then ye shall bring a sheaf of
the firstfruits of your harvest unto the priest:

And he shall wave the sheaf before the LORD, to be
accepted for you: on the morrow after the sabbath the
priest shall wave it.

And ye shall offer that day when ye wave the sheaf
an he lamb without blemish of the first year for a burnt
offering unto the LORD.

And the meat offering thereof *shall be* two tenth deals
of fine flour mingled with oil, an offering made by fire
unto the LORD *for* a sweet savour: and the drink offering
thereof *shall be* of wine, the fourth *part* of an hin.

And ye shall eat neither bread, nor parched corn, nor
green ears, until the selfsame day that ye have brought
an offering unto your God: *it shall be* a statute for ever
throughout your generations in all your dwellings.

(Leviticus 23:9-14)

Jesus died on Passover and was buried on Unleavened Bread, then raised
on First Fruits, no great gift has God given man than His Son to die on the
cross. Each feast of the LORD's symbolizes an action of our Lord's life as
we will soon find out, some yet to be fulfilled in the fall feasts.

But now is Christ risen from the dead, *and* become the
firstfruits of them that slept.

For since by man *came* death, by man *came* also the
resurrection of the dead.

For as in Adam all die, even so in Christ shall all be
made alive.

But every man in his own order: Christ the firstfruits;
afterward they that are Christ's at his coming.

(1 Corinthians 15:20-23)

First Fruits marked the start of Israel's grain harvest and the beginning of
the count for the Feast of Weeks (Pentecost), Israel's forth feast. The Feast of
Weeks took place forty nine days after First Fruits on the Fiftieth Day; and
demonstrates to man that God is owner of everything. He has given us the
ability to attain success by returning to Him the "first" of our produce. God

declared that the first fruits on the land was His, including the firstborn of livestock. Even the Donkey was required to be redeemed. (Ex. 22:29, 23:19, 34:26, Dt. 18:4, 26:2) The firstborn son was also to be redeemed according to the law. Jesus was presented in the temple to fulfill this verse.

> Every thing devoted in Israel shall be thine.
>
> Every thing that openeth the matrix in all flesh, which they bring unto the LORD, *whether it be* of men or beasts, shall be thine: nevertheless the firstborn of man shalt thou surely redeem, and the firstling of unclean beasts shalt thou redeem.
>
> And those that are to be redeemed from a month old shalt thou redeem, according to thine estimation, for the money of five shekels, after the shekel of the sanctuary, which *is* twenty gerahs.
>
> But the firstling of a cow, or the firstling of a sheep, or the firstling of a goat, thou shalt not redeem; they *are* holy: thou shalt sprinkle their blood upon the altar, and shalt burn their fat *for* an offering made by fire, for a sweet savour unto the LORD.
>
> And the flesh of them shall be thine, as the wave breast and as the right shoulder are thine.
>
> All the heave offerings of the holy things, which the children of Israel offer unto the LORD, have I given thee, and thy sons and thy daughters with thee, by a statute for ever: it *is* a covenant of salt for ever before the LORD unto thee and to thy seed with thee.
>
> (Numbers 18:14-19)

THE FEAST OF PENTECOST

Festival of Weeks

And ye shall count unto you from the morrow after the sabbath, from the day that ye brought the sheaf of the wave offering; seven sabbaths shall be complete:

Even unto the morrow after the seventh sabbath shall ye number fifty days; and ye shall offer a new meat offering unto the LORD.

Ye shall bring out of your habitations two wave loaves of two tenth deals: they shall be of fine flour; they shall be baken with leaven; *they are* the firstfruits unto the LORD.

And ye shall offer with the bread seven lambs without blemish of the first year, and one young bullock, and two rams: they shall be *for* a burnt offering unto the LORD, with their meat offering, and their drink offerings, *even* an offering made by fire, of sweet savour unto the LORD.

Then ye shall sacrifice one kid of the goats for a sin offering, and two lambs of the first year for a sacrifice of peace offerings.

And the priest shall wave them with the bread of the firstfruits *for* a wave offering before the LORD, with the two lambs: they shall be holy to the LORD for the priest.

And ye shall proclaim on the selfsame day, *that* it may be an holy convocation unto you: ye shall do no servile work *therein: it shall be* a statute for ever in all your dwellings throughout your generations.

And when ye reap the harvest of your land, thou shalt not make clean riddance of the corners of thy field when thou reapest, neither shalt thou gather any gleaning of thy harvest: thou shalt leave them unto the poor, and to the stranger: I *am* the LORD your God.

(Leviticus 23:15-22)

"Pentecost" is an English word meaning "Fifty" in the Greek "*pentekostos*", which means "fifty." It comes from the ancient Christian expression pentekoste hemera, which means "fiftieth day." This holy day was known as the Festival of Weeks, or, more simply, Weeks (*Shavuot* in Hebrew). *Shavuot* was the second of three compulsory pilgrimage feast in Israel's yearly cycle of holy days. It was originally a harvest festival.

And ye shall count unto you from the morrow after the sabbath, from the day that ye brought the sheaf of the wave offering; seven sabbaths shall be complete:

Even unto the morrow after the seventh sabbath shall ye number fifty days; and ye shall offer a new meat offering unto the LORD.

(Leviticus 23:15-16)

And the feast of harvest, the firstfruits of thy labours, which thou hast sown in the field: and the feast of ingathering, *which is* in the end of the year, when thou hast gathered in thy labours out of the field.

(Exodus 23:16)

Shavuot/Pentecost later became a day to commemorate the giving of the law on Mr. Sinai. Pentecost is especially special for Christians today because seven weeks after the resurrection of Jesus, during the Jewish feast of Shavuot/Pentecost, the Holy Spirit was poured out upon the disciples, His very first followers, empowering them for their mission and the church was born with 3000 souls added. Peter preached his first sermon interpreting the prophet Joel.

And when the day of Pentecost was fully come, they were all with one accord in one place.

And suddenly there came a sound from heaven as of a rushing mighty wind, and it filled all the house where they were sitting.

And there appeared unto them cloven tongues like as of fire, and it sat upon each of them.

And they were all filled with the Holy Ghost, and began to speak with other tongues, as the Spirit gave them utterance.

(Acts 2:1-4)

But Peter, standing up with the eleven, lifted up his voice, and said unto them, Ye men of Judaea, and all *ye* that dwell at Jerusalem, be this known unto you, and hearken to my words:

For these are not drunken, as ye suppose, seeing it is *but* the third hour of the day.

But this is that which was spoken by the prophet Joel;

And it shall come to pass in the last days, saith God, I will pour out of my Spirit upon all flesh: and your sons and your daughters shall prophesy, and your young men shall see visions, and your old men shall dream dreams:

And on my servants and on my handmaidens I will pour out in those days of my Spirit; and they shall prophesy:

(Acts 2:14-18)

Peter preaches our Messiah crucified, risen and the worker of miracles. The King and Lord of all, the living beloved Son of God, who was and is and is to come. Jesus said:

And, behold, I come quickly; and my reward *is* with me, to give every man according as his work shall be.
I am Alpha and Omega, the beginning and the end, the first and the last.

Blessed *are* they that do his commandments, that they may have right to the tree of life, and may enter in through the gates into the city.

(Revelation 22:12-14)

- The Holy Spirit helps us to confess Jesus as Lord

Wherefore I give you to understand, that no man speaking by the Spirit of God calleth Jesus accursed:

(1 Corinthians 12:3)

- Empowers us to serve God with supernatural power

Now there are diversities of gifts, but the same Spirit.

And there are differences of administrations, but the same Lord.

And there are diversities of operations, but it is the same God which worketh all in all.

But the manifestation of the Spirit is given to every man to profit withal.

For to one is given by the Spirit the word of wisdom; to another the word of knowledge by the same Spirit;

To another faith by the same Spirit; to another the gifts of healing by the same Spirit;

To another the working of miracles; to another prophecy; to another discerning of spirits; to another *divers* kinds of tongues; to another the interpretation of tongues:

But all these worketh that one and the selfsame Spirit, dividing to every man severally as he will.

(1 Corinthians 12:4-11)

- Binds us together as the body of Christ

For as the body is one, and hath many members, and all the members of that one body, being many, are one body: so also *is* Christ.

For by one Spirit are we all baptized into one body, whether *we be* Jews or Gentiles, whether *we be* bond or free; and have been all made to drink into one Spirit.

1 Corinthians 12:12-13)

- Helps us to pray

Likewise the Spirit also helpeth our infirmities: for we know not what we should pray for as we ought: but the Spirit itself maketh intercession for us with groanings which cannot be uttered.

(Romans 8:26)

- Intercedes for us with God the Father

And he that searcheth the hearts knoweth what *is* the mind of the Spirit, because he maketh intercession for the saints according to *the will of* God.

(Romans 8:27)

- The spirit guides us

  If we live in the Spirit, let us also walk in the Spirit.
  (Galatians 5:25)

- Helping us to live like Jesus

  But the fruit of the Spirit is love, joy, peace, longsuffering, gentleness, goodness, faith,
  Meekness, temperance: against such there is no law.
  (Galatians 5:22-23)

On the Day of Pentecost Jesus sent the Comforter, the Holy Spirit to give us power to live for Him. The Holy Spirit helps us witness and guides us in our Christian walk with Jesus.

THE FALL FEASTS

The last 3 feasts are prophetic, yet to be fulfilled by Jesus, they are Rosh Hashanah (Trumpets), Atonement and Tabernacles. Because Jesus fulfilled the first four feasts on the actual feast days, it is safe to believe that the last three will be fulfilled on the actual feast days.

ROSH HASHANAH

Rosh Hashanah or Jewish New Year is also called the Feast of Trumpets in the Bible because it begins the Jewish New Year. There are several names for Rosh Hashanah some of which are:

- Day No Man Knows
- Yom Teruah
- Day of the Awakening
- Day the Doors opened in Heaven

And the LORD spake unto Moses, saying,

Speak unto the children of Israel, saying, In the seventh month, in the first *day* of the month, shall ye have a sabbath, a memorial of blowing of trumpets, an holy convocation.

Ye shall do no servile work *therein*: but ye shall offer an offering made by fire unto the LORD.

(Leviticus 23:23-25)

HIGH HOLY DAYS

The High Holidays begin with Rosh Hashanah (הנשה שאר), which translates from Hebrew as "the head of the year." it is generally referred to as *the Jewish New Year*.

It is observed for two days starting on the 1ˢᵗ of Tishrei, the seventh month of the Hebrew calendar, usually in September. Tishrei is the first month of the Jewish civil year, but the seventh month of the ecclesiastical year. In Jewish tradition, Rosh Hashanah marks…

- The anniversary of the creation of the world as described in the Torah.
- Beginning of a 10-day period on the Jewish calendar that focuses on repentance or *teshuvah*.
- Jews mark the holy day with festive meals and prayer services and greetings to one aother *L'shanah tovah tikateiv v'techateim*, which means "May you be inscribed and sealed for a good year."
- Ten Days of Repentance (or Days of Awe) with the blowing of the ram's horn, the shofar, calling God's people together to repent from their sins.
- During Rosh Hashanah synagogue services, the trumpet traditionally sounds 100 notes.

Eschatologists consider ROSH HASHANAH (Yom Teruah) the most likely day that Jesus Christ will return for the church, only they cannot discern during which year. ROSH HASHANAH is called "The Day That No-One Knows". It is the only feast/festival day that falls on the first day of a month.

I also believe this is the day the Lord returns for His Bride (the church). We do not know the exact time but we can know it is drawing near. Jesus has given us signs that we may know and be ready for His return (the Rapture).

> Behold, I shew you a mystery; We shall not all sleep, but we shall all be changed,
> In a moment, in the twinkling of an eye, at the last trump: for the trumpet shall sound, and the dead shall be raised incorruptible, and we shall be changed.
>
> (1 Corinthians 15:51-52)

> And when he had spoken these things, while they beheld, he was taken up; and a cloud received him out of their sight.
> And while they looked stedfastly toward heaven as he went up, behold, two men stood by them in white apparel;
> Which also said, Ye men of Galilee, why stand ye gazing up into heaven? this same Jesus, which is taken up from you into heaven, shall so come in like manner as ye have seen him go into heaven.
>
> (Acts 1:9-11)

> For the Lord himself shall descend from heaven with a shout, with the voice of the archangel, and with the trump of God: and the dead in Christ shall rise first:
>
> (1 Thessalonians 4:16)

> Behold, I shew you a mystery; We shall not all sleep, but we shall all be changed,
> In a moment, in the twinkling of an eye, at the last trump: for the trumpet shall sound, and the dead shall be raised incorruptible, and we shall be changed.
> For this corruptible must put on incorruption, and this mortal *must* put on immortality.
> So when this corruptible shall have put on incorruption, and this mortal shall have put on immortality, then shall be brought to pass the saying that is written, Death is swallowed up in victory.

O death, where *is* thy sting? O grave, where *is* thy victory?
The sting of death *is* sin; and the strength of sin *is* the law.
But thanks *be* to God, which giveth us the victory
through our Lord Jesus Christ.

(1 Corinthians 15:51-57)

JESUS WILL RETURN FOR HIS CHURCH! Rosh Hashanah yet to be fulfilled by Jesus.

The days between Rosh Hashanah and Day of Atonement are called **Days of Awe or (Teshuva).**

Many tragedies have happened to Israel during this time period. Here are just some:

- God being displeased with Israel's refusal of going into the promised land, that generation never entered except for Caleb and Joshua
- 1st Temple destroyed 423 BC
- Massacre of Betar 133 BC
- 2nd Temple destroyed 69 BC
- Jews expelled from Spain March 31, 1492

Did you know Columbus was a Jew, who came to America 1492, he was expelled from Spain and set out to search for a new world?

THE DAY OF ATONEMENT YOM YIPPUR

And the LORD spake unto Moses, saying,
Also on the tenth *day* of this seventh month *there shall be* a day of atonement: it shall be an holy convocation unto you; and ye shall afflict your souls, and offer an offering made by fire unto the LORD.
And ye shall do no work in that same day: for it *is* a day of atonement.

(Leviticus 23:26-28)

YOM KIPPUR is the Day of Atonement, the day when one is to afflict their soul to remember, confess and repent-of the sins committed during the previous year. And, when or where appropriate, to make amends to those harmed by those sins. This is one of the most important days for the Jews.

> Therefore if thou bring thy gift to the altar, and there rememberest that thy brother hath ought against thee;
> Leave there thy gift before the altar, and go thy way; first be reconciled to thy brother, and then come and offer thy gift.
>
> (Matthew 5:23-24)

THE FEAST OF TABENACLES
FEAST OF INGATHERING

Also known as "Feast of Ingathering" and the "Feast of Booths". The Israelites were required to leave their homes and set up booths or tents made with branches with holes in the roof so that the stars would be seen at night. This was to bring to their remembrance the time they left Egypt and lived in the wilderness on their way to Canaan.

> And the feast of harvest, the firstfruits of thy labours, which thou hast sown in the field: and the feast of ingathering, *which is* in the end of the year, when thou hast gathered in thy labours out of the field.
>
> (Exodus 23:16)

> And thou shalt observe the feast of weeks, of the firstfruits of wheat harvest, and the feast of ingathering at the year's end.
>
> (Exodus 34:22)

> Thou shalt observe the feast of tabernacles seven days, after that thou hast gathered in thy corn and thy wine:
> And thou shalt rejoice in thy feast, thou, and thy son, and thy daughter, and thy manservant, and thy

maidservant, and the Levite, the stranger, and the fatherless, and the widow, that *are* within thy gates.

(Deuteronomy 16:13-14)

This feast looks forward to the Millennial Reign of Christ after the Great Tribulation Period, when Jesus Christ will rule and reign with saints and people that made it through the tribulation period. There will be people who come out of the tribulation period and live in the 1000 year reign of Jesus Christ.

The fulfilment of this feast will be when God will once again dwell or "tabernacle" with His people in the millennium.

> And it shall come to pass, *that* every one that is left of all the nations which came against Jerusalem shall even go up from year to year to worship the King, the LORD of hosts, and to keep the feast of tabernacles.
>
> And it shall be, *that* whoso will not come up of *all* the families of the earth unto Jerusalem to worship the King, the LORD of hosts, even upon them shall be no rain.
>
> And if the family of Egypt go not up, and come not, that *have* no *rain*; there shall be the plague, wherewith the LORD will smite the heathen that come not up to keep the feast of tabernacles.
>
> This shall be the punishment of Egypt, and the punishment of all nations that come not up to keep the feast of tabernacles.
>
> (Zechariah 14:16-19)

> And I saw an angel come down from heaven, having the key of the bottomless pit and a great chain in his hand.
>
> And he laid hold on the dragon, that old serpent, which is the Devil, and Satan, and bound him a thousand years,
>
> And cast him into the bottomless pit, and shut him up, and set a seal upon him, that he should deceive the nations no more, till the thousand years should be fulfilled: and after that he must be loosed a little season.

And I saw thrones, and they sat upon them, and judgment was given unto them: and *I saw* the souls of them that were beheaded for the witness of Jesus, and for the word of God, and which had not worshipped the beast, neither his image, neither had received *his* mark upon their foreheads, or in their hands; and they lived and reigned with Christ a thousand years.

(Revelation 20:1-4)

I hope this book has been helpful to you in better understanding the Bible and God's plan of salvation. I have tried to touch on a few highlights of the life of Jesus and how He has fulfilled God's plan from His birth to His death and that Jesus will fulfill the last of God's appointed times as we move forward. Remember the Lord always, repent, love and serve Him daily that ye may enter into His peace and rest and rejoice at His coming.

REFERENCES

ASKELM.com/star, The Star of Bethlehem by Dr. Ernest Martin, charter 5, 8

Edersheim, Alfred. The Temple: Its Ministry and Services as they were at the Time of Jesus Christ. Hendrickson Publishers, 1994

Edersheim, Alfred. The Life and Times of Jesus the Messiah. Hendrickson Publishers, 1993.

Holy Bible: King James Version

Joseph Lenard. Mysteries of Jesus' Life Revealed. info@truthinscripture.net.

Steven Rudd. steve.rudd@bible.ca by Warren E. Berkley

Barnes, Albert. Barnes' Notes on the New Testament. Edited by Robert Frew

Clarke, Adam. Adam Clarke's Commentary. New York: Abingdon-Cokesbury Press, 1826.

Edersheim, Alfred. Bible History Old Testament. London: Religious Tract Society, 1890.

Edersheim, Alfred (1825-1889). Sketches of Jewish Social Life in the Days of Christ. London: The Religious Tract Society, 1876.

Josephus, Flavius. The Works of Flavius Josephus. Translated by William Whiston. Hartford, CN: S. S. Scranton, 1905.

Keener, Craig S. The IVP Bible Background Commentary – New Testament. Downers Grove, IL: InterVarsity Press, 1993.

Richards, Lawrence O. The Teacher's Commentary. Wheaton, IL: Victor Books, 1987.

Smith, William. Smith's Bible Dictionary: Comprising Antiquities, Biography, Geography, Natural History. Archaeology and Literature Philadelphia: A.J. Holman & Co., 1901.

Strong, James. Strong's Talking Greek & Hebrew Dictionary. Austin, TX: Corp., 2007.

Water, Mark. comp. Encyclopedia of Jesus' Life and Time. Chattanooga, TN: AMG Publishers, 2005.

Wight, Fred H. Manners and Customs of Bible Lands. Chicago: Moody press, 1980.

Printed in the United States
By Bookmasters